THE HUNTING & FISHING LIBRARY®

FISHING RIVERS & STREAMS

By Dick Sternberg

DICK STERNBERG is a nationally known river-fishing authority. Much of his career as a professional fisheries biologist has been devoted to studying big rivers; much of his angling career to fishing them.

CY DECOSSE INCORPORATED
Chairman: Cy DeCosse
President: James B. Maus
Executive Vice President: William B. Jones

FISHING RIVERS & STREAMS
Author and Project Director: Dick Sternberg
Editor: Greg Breining
Project Manager: Joseph Cella
Art Director: Bradley Springer
Principal Photographer: William Lindner
Photo Directors: Joseph Cella, Eric Lindberg
Photo Assistants: Todd Guerrero, Mike Hehner, Jim Moynagh
Research Supervisor: Eric Lindberg
Researchers: Todd Guerrero, Mike Hehner, Jim Moynagh
Production Manager: Jim Bindas
Assistant Production Managers: Julie Churchill, Amelia Merz
Typesetting: Kevin D. Frakes, Linda Schloegel
Production Staff: Janice Cauley, Sheila DiPaola, Joe Fahey, Mark Jacobson, Yelena Konrardy, Scott Lamoureux, David Schelitzche, Nik Wogstad
Illustrators: Thomas Boll, Yelena Konrardy, Jon Q. Wright
Contributing Photographers: Kim Baily; Joseph Cella; Dick Christie, Jim Glenn/South Carolina Wildlife and Marine Resources Dept.; Lenny Frasure; Dan Guravich; Tim Haske/ProFiles West; Mike Hehner; Mark Macemon; Dan Meyers; Mark Miller; Chuck Nields; Steve Olson; John W. Robinson/Missouri Department of Conservation; Dick Sternberg; Marty Wencek
Cooperating Individuals and Agencies: W.L. Ammons; Arkansas Game and Fish Commission — Keith Sutton; Avon Marine; Max Bachhuber; Brad Ballard; Bear's Den Lodge — Art Barefoot; James Bodiford; Bernie Bogenref; Rudolph Bone; Joe Bucher; Ken Clark; George Collins; Bill Conley; Jerry Cox; Robert Desrocher; Ernie Erickson; Gene Flynn; Keith Flynn; Lenny Frasure; Butch Furtman; Mark Galliger; Dan Gapen; Georgia Dept. of Natural Resources — Carl Hall; Hoot Gibson; Larry Gilbert; Dick Grzywinski; Happy Hooker Excursions — Steve Wieber; Mark Herrin; Eugene S. Hood; Bill Houle; Idaho Fish and Game Dept. — Bert Bowler, Ed Buettner, Keith Kiler, Jim Lukans, Steve Pittet; In Season Adventures, Inc. — Pat Gavin, Bob Knoop, Carl Salling; Rudolph Inman; Jackson Clarion Ledger — Bobby Cleveland; Jim's Bait — Jim Keuten; Tony Kinton; Sue Lanier; Ray Mertes; Minnesota Dept. of Natural Resources — Larry Gates, Gary Grunwald, Don Schliep; Mississippi Dept. of Economic Development — Jay Hambright, John Horhn; Mississippi Dept. of Wildlife Conservation — John Burriss, Henry Follmer, Tom Holman, Tommy Robinson; Mississippi State University — Don Jackson; Tom Nightengale; North Carolina Dept. of Natural Resources — Jim Davis; Ontario Ministry of Natural Resources — Ed Chevrette, Ken Jackson, John Thompson; Ontario Ministry of Tourism & Recreation — Tom Adamchick; Oregon State University — Henry L. Pittock; Scott Palmer; Marty Papke; Steve Payne; Bill Petit; Tom Pfister; Ralph Phillips; Bob Ponds; Q-M Bait — Troy Bell; R & R Marine; S & S Outfitters — John Patterson; Peter Schennach; Scribbs Institute of Oceanography — Dr. Ron Flick; Jim Sessions; Shakopee Marine Service; South Carolina Wildlife and Marine Resources Dept. — Dave Allen, Dick Christie, Bruce Stender; Harry Stiles; Robert Talbert; Texas Parks and Wildlife Dept.; Tony Thomson; Thorne Brothers — Greg Thorne; University of Washington — Alyn C. Duxbury; Virginia Institute of Marine Sciences — Dr. John Rusecki; Voyageur's North — Tom Terry; Wisconsin Dept. of Natural Resources; Rich Zaleski
Cooperating Manufacturers: Abu-Garcia, Inc.; Bass Pro Shops; Bass'n Man Lure Co.; Berkley, Inc./Trilene Fishing Line; Bill Lewis Lures; Bill Norman Lures, Inc.; Bomber Bait Company; Brell Mar Products, Inc.; Bullet Weights, Inc.; Classic Mfg./Culprit Lures; D & K Distributors, Inc.; Daiwa Corporation; Feldman Eng. & Mfg. Co., Inc.; Furuno USA, Inc.; GNB, Incorporated/Stowaway Batteries; The Gaines Company; Garland Lures, Inc.; Herrick Enterprises/Wave Wackers; Hondex Marine Electronics; John J. Hildebrandt Corporation; Johnson Fishing, Inc.; Koden International, Inc.; LaCrosse Footwear, Inc.; Lowe Boats; Lowrance Electronics, Inc.; Mercury Marine/Mariner Outboards; Mister Twister, Inc.; Nordic Crestliner Boat Co.; Normark Corporation; Pointmatic Corporation; Rebel Lures; River Rat Lure Company; Scorcher Bait Co., Inc.; Sheldon's, Inc.; Si-Tex Marine Electronics, Inc.; Slater's Jigs; Snag Proof Manufacturing, Inc.; St. Croix Rod Co.; Stanley Jigs, Inc.; Stearns Manufacturing Company; Stren Fishing Line; Uncle Josh Bait Company; VMC, Inc.; Wright & McGill Company; Yakima Bait Company; Yamaha Motor Corp., USA
Color Separations: Scantrans Pte. Ltd.
Printing: R. R. Donnelley & Sons Co. (0190)

Also available from the publisher: *The Art of Freshwater Fishing, Cleaning & Cooking Fish, Fishing With Live Bait, Largemouth Bass, Panfish, The Art of Hunting, Fishing With Artificial Lures, Walleye, Smallmouth Bass, Dressing & Cooking Wild Game, Freshwater Gamefish of North America, Fishing Update No. I, Trout, Secrets of the Fishing Pros*

Library of Congress
Cataloging-in-Publication Data

Sternberg, Dick
Fishing rivers & streams/by Dick Sternberg
p.c.m. — (The Hunting & fishing library)
ISBN 0-86573-031-8
1. Fishing — United States. 2. Fishing — Canada.
3. Fishes, Freshwater — United States. 4. Fishes, Freshwater — Canada. I. Title. II. Title: Fishing rivers and streams. III. series.
SH463.S74 1990   89-23707
799.1' 10973 — dc20   CIP

Contents

Introduction 4

Understanding Rivers & Streams 6
  Rivers & Streams: The Basics 8
  Current Speed 10
  Cover 12
  Water Temperature 18
  Food 22
  How Streams Change 24
  Fluctuating Water Levels 26
  Threats to Stream Habitat 28
  River Navigation 30

Fishing Rivers & Streams 36

  Midwestern Mainstem Rivers 38
    Case Study: Upper Mississippi River,
    Minnesota & Wisconsin 40
      Walleyes & Saugers 46
      Bluegills & Crappies 50
      Largemouth Bass 54
      Smallmouth Bass 56
      Northern Pike 58
      White Bass 60
      Catfish 62

  Tidewater Rivers 64
    Case Study: Cooper River, South Carolina . . 67
    Sunfish 70
    Largemouth Bass 74
    Catfish 78
    Striped Bass 80
    Shad 82
    Other Species 84

Southern Largemouth Rivers 86
  Case Study: Pearl River, Mississippi 88
    Largemouth Bass 90
    Spotted Bass 94
    Wipers 96
    Crappies 98
    Catfish 100

Northern Smallmouth Streams 102
  Case Study: St. Louis River,
  Minnesota 104
    Smallmouth Bass 106
    Northern Pike 109
    Walleyes 110
    Catfish 112

Canadian Trophy Pike Rivers 114
  Case Study: Attawapiskat River, Ontario . . . 116
    Northern Pike 120
    Walleyes 124

Western Corridor Rivers 126
  Case Study: Snake River, Idaho,
  Oregon & Washington 128
    Steelhead & Rainbow Trout 132
    Smallmouth Bass 136
    White Sturgeon 138

Great Lakes Tributaries 142
  Case Study: French River, Ontario 144
    Walleyes 146
    Muskies 148
    Smallmouth Bass 152
    Northern Pike 154

Index 156

Introduction

North America is blessed with an abundance of flowing water. There are 3.25 million miles of rivers and streams in the United States alone — enough to circle the globe 130 times. Yet, more than two-thirds of our fishing is done in lakes.

Most anglers are intimidated by moving water; they don't know where to find fish or how to catch them. The purpose of this book is to improve your river-fishing skills.

The book focuses on warmwater rivers and streams. Compared to trout streams, these waters have been forgotten by the outdoor press, even though they make up a much greater percentage of North America's total stream mileage.

One reason for the inattention: it's difficult to say much in general about warmwater streams; they vary from trickles only a few feet across to great rivers such as the Mississippi. Some support only one or two species of gamefish; others, a dozen or more. And the techniques for fishing these streams are as diverse as the streams themselves.

In the first part of the book, "Understanding Rivers and Streams," we'll show you how current speed, water temperature, cover and food determine where the fish will be in any river or stream. We'll also explain how changing water levels affect fish location. Without this knowledge, finding fish would be strictly guesswork.

It would be impossible to show you exactly where to find fish and how to catch them in every conceivable type of warmwater stream, so we've organized the second part of the book, "Fishing Rivers and Streams," into a series of case studies that represent most of the river-fishing situations anglers are likely to encounter.

Each case study gives you all necessary information for fishing a river of that type, from the equipment needed to the exact techniques and lures used for each species of gamefish. Detailed maps will show you the type of habitat where every important species is likely to be found in each season. You'll even learn the tricks that help local experts catch fish when nobody else can.

Even though you may never fish the streams featured in the case studies, the studies can be applied to your favorite waters. If you live on the East Coast, for instance, you're probably not too far from a good tidewater river. The case study featuring South Carolina's Cooper River will give you most of the information you need for fishing practically any tidewater river on the Eastern Seaboard.

Other case studies may also give you some ideas for fishing your favorite streams. A smallmouth bass method used on a midwestern mainstem river, for instance, will probably work equally well on a western corridor river.

Warmwater rivers and streams are the last frontier of freshwater fishing. This book will help you take advantage of the phenomenal fishing opportunity that these waters have to offer.

Understanding
Rivers & Streams

Rivers & Streams: The Basics

To an angler who does most of his fishing in lakes, river fishing is frustrating. Fish behave differently in moving water than in still water, and unless you understand these differences and alter your techniques accordingly, you'll spend a lot of discouraging hours on the water.

But river fishing is not necessarily tougher than lake fishing — it's just different.

In rivers, conditions are constantly changing. A heavy rain can transform a gently gurgling stream into a raging torrent within hours. You must know how to adjust to changes in water level, clarity and current speed.

On the other hand, streams can be forgiving. When a cold front shuts down the fishing in a lake, stream fish continue to bite. They also seem less affected by changes in air temperature and cloud cover.

River fish have the same basic needs as any other fish. Besides water of the right temperature, they need adequate cover and a dependable food supply. Although they live in a river, they spend very little of their time in fast water. Fighting the current takes too much energy.

Instead, they use the current to their advantage. Most river fish lie behind a boulder or in some other slack-water pocket, waiting for an insect or unsuspecting minnow to drift past them. Then they dart into the current, grab the morsel, and return to their lie — all within a few seconds. And once they find a comfortable lie, they tend to stay put.

Lake fish spend more time searching for food. They comb the shorelines and reefs, sometimes moving from deep to shallow water several times a day. Where you find them one day has little bearing on where they'll be the next.

In this respect, river fishermen have an advantage, assuming they know how to read the water and spot the lies. This chapter will show you what to look for.

By learning how much current different fish species will tolerate, you'll know what type of water is most likely to hold them. Tolerances vary widely, even between closely related species. This explains why they're found in different types of habitat. A smallmouth bass, for instance, will tolerate considerably more current than a largemouth; a muskie, more than a northern pike.

After you learn how to recognize the right type of water, you can concentrate on finding the slack-water pockets likely to hold gamefish. We'll point out many different kinds, some obvious and some not so obvious.

This chapter will also help you understand the importance of water temperature in finding fish, and how the food supply affects the type and quantity of fish a stream can produce. You'll learn how streams change from day to day, from season to season, and over the long term, and how these changes affect your fishing strategy. We'll also show you some of the environmental problems affecting rivers and streams, and give you some pointers on river navigation.

Once you learn these basics and spend some time fishing moving water, you'll be as comfortable as you would be on your favorite lake.

Current Speed

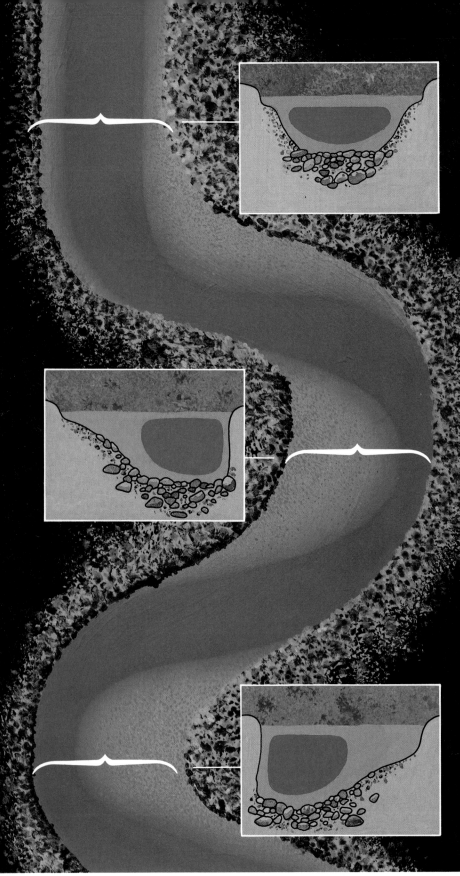

CHANNEL LOCATION depends on the configuration of the stream. Where the stream is straight, the channel is in the middle. As the stream turns, the channel shifts to the outside bends. The cross sections show the depths of the channel and the zones of fastest current (dark blue). Current is slower on the surface, on the bottom and along the sides because of friction with the air and the streambed.

How fast the water is moving determines what type of fish can live in a stream. Current speed depends mainly on the *gradient*, or slope, of the streambed, the shape of the channel and the amount of flow.

A stream that drops rapidly in elevation along its course is called a high-gradient stream. One that drops very little is a low-gradient stream. The higher the gradient, the faster the current. Typically, a stream's gradient is highest near the source. But as the stream flows along, sediment is deposited, gradually flattening the streambed and slowing the current.

Current-Speed Tolerances

SPECIES	CURRENT SPEED*
Steelhead	fast
Smallmouth bass	med. fast
Walleye	medium
Sauger	medium
Muskie	medium
Spotted bass	medium
Channel catfish	medium
White sturgeon	medium
Striped bass	medium
Shad	medium
Wiper	medium
Largemouth bass	slow
Northern pike	slow
Flathead catfish	slow
Blue catfish	slow
White bass	slow
Black, white crappies	slow
Bluegill	slow
Redear sunfish	slow

*These current speeds are relative; no fish are found in the fastest water.

Normally, the gradient and current speed are lowest near the mouth.

In a given stream, current speed generally increases as the flow picks up. The current also speeds up when the channel narrows or shallows up because the same amount of water is forced through a smaller passage.

When the current increases, it excavates a deep *pool*. The current in the pool is slower, so much of the sediment carried by the water settles out. As the sediment builds up, the water gets shallower and the current speeds up, forming a *riffle*. The fast water then starts to dig the channel deeper, creating a *run*. This process continues to repeat itself along the stream course, accounting for the typical pool-riffle-run configuration of many small streams. Larger streams may have a pool-riffle-run configuration as well, but this pattern is harder to see in a larger expanse of water.

Because sediment settles out in slow current, pools have fine bottom materials, such as sand, silt or muck. Current flows smoothly over this type of bottom, so the surface appears flat. In riffles and runs, where the current is swift, sediment washes away, leaving coarse materials such as gravel, rocks and boulders. Large rocks and boulders deflect the current, producing a turbulent flow.

Fish behave much differently in fast current than in slow. Where the current is fast, fish are conditioned to grab food quickly, without much examination. Otherwise, the current would sweep it away. This explains why fish in fast water are quicker to take a lure than those in slow water. Fish are also easier to locate in fast water. Instead of scattering throughout the stream, they're confined to specific slack-water areas, where they can avoid the fast current.

Anyone who has ever navigated a small river knows that you must motor along the outside bends to stay in deep water. As explained on the opposite page, the deepest, fastest part of the stream always follows the outside bends. Expert stream fishermen can spot this deep zone at a glance; they know that most stream species hang in it or alongside it.

How Gradient Determines Which Fish Species Live in a Stream

CURRENT

HIGH-GRADIENT areas have the fastest current and largest boulders; they hold current-tolerant species such as smallmouth bass. The higher the gradient, the more closely fish hug bottom to escape the current.

MEDIUM-GRADIENT areas have moderate current and smaller rocks and gravel; they hold fish such as walleyes and channel catfish. Fish stay near bottom, but not as close as in fast current.

LOW-GRADIENT areas have slow current and a bottom of silt, sand or muck; they hold slow-water species such as largemouth bass and sunfish. Because of the slow current, fish can cruise farther off bottom.

ROUND BOULDERS have eddies on both the upstream and downstream sides. The eddy that forms downstream of the boulder (right) is larger and usually holds the most fish. But the upstream eddy (left), formed

Cover

Stream fish learn to seek cover starting the moment they hatch. The tiny fry are weak swimmers, and unless they can hide behind a pebble or some other type of cover, they are swept away by the current. Cover is also needed to conceal the fry from larger fish and predaceous insects.

Fish need larger pieces of cover to shade and conceal them as they grow. The biggest fish usually seek out the largest boulders and logs or the deepest undercuts. Water that lacks this type of cover will probably hold only small fish.

As discussed earlier, fish species differ in their current tolerances (p. 10). Generally, those that are well adapted to current will hold in a smaller pocket of slack water than those that are primarily lake dwellers. For a smallmouth bass, a single branch extending into the current may provide enough cover. But a crappie requires a good-sized pool or eddy.

Streams that *meander*, or wind, usually have more cover than streams with relatively straight channels. Meandering streams generally have a pool-riffle-run

by water deflecting off the boulder's face, may also hold a fish or two. Most fishermen are aware of the eddy on the downstream side, but many fail to recognize the one on the upstream side.

configuration with plenty of deep holes and undercut banks. A stream with a straight channel usually lacks the pool-riffle-run configuration, and the depth is fairly uniform throughout. Cover for adult fish is in short supply.

The best cover not only breaks the current, but also provides overhead protection. Consequently, fish prefer slack water beneath an undercut bank to an eddy behind a boulder.

Every stream has a few prime pieces of cover that some anglers refer to as "fish magnets." Usually, these spots are occupied by one or two of the stream's largest, most dominant fish. When one of these fish

is caught, another of about the same size moves in to replace it. The most consistently successful anglers on a stream are those who know several of these spots.

Good cover is not always easy to recognize. You can easily spot a half-submerged boulder or a fallen tree, but some types of eddies and slack-water pockets are difficult to see. With a little practice, however, you'll learn to recognize the subtle visual clues that reveal their location.

On the following pages are the most common types of eddies and slack-water areas likely to hold river gamefish.

STREAMLINED BOULDERS have an eddy on the downstream side only. Water flows smoothly over the front of the boulder, so no upstream eddy is formed.

BOILS form when water deflects off of submerged objects, such as boulders. An eddy forms below the boulder, several feet *upstream* of the boil.

POINT-BARS form along inside bends, where slow current allows sediment to settle out. Eddies below point-bars are the prime fish-holding zones in many streams.

POINTS or sharp bends in the river create major eddies. The longer the point or sharper the bend, the larger the eddy that will form.

BRIDGE PILINGS have eddies on the upstream and downstream ends. Often, the cover is better than it looks because of riprap piled at the base to reduce erosion.

NOTCHES in the shoreline or along the side of an island create small slack-water pockets that often go unnoticed by anglers.

LOGJAMS sometimes block the entire channel of a river, creating a large eddy downstream and sometimes deflecting enough current to the side to cut a new channel.

WING DAMS, man-made current deflectors, create eddies on both the upstream and downstream sides. Often, current swirling around the end cuts a deep hole.

CHANNEL MARKERS built on rock piles make excellent fishing spots. The rock pile not only forms an eddy, it also attracts minnows, crayfish and other fish food.

DUNES often develop on a shifting sand bottom. Current brushes the peaks of the dunes, but a slack-water pocket forms below each dune.

TRIBUTARY JUNCTIONS are often good fishing spots because the delta of the inflowing stream creates an eddy downstream of the entry point.

POOLS are slow-moving, deep areas with a slick surface. When viewed from above, the water looks darker than the surrounding water.

15

WEEDBEDS create diverse current patterns. Fish lie in slow water in the beds themselves; they dart out to grab food drifting through channels between the beds.

ROOTED WEED CLUMPS often develop a mound of sediment around the base. An eddy then forms on the downstream side, digging out a hole.

TAILWATER EDDIES form along the sides of the fast current below a dam. Sometimes the reverse current in the eddy is nearly as strong as the mainstream current.

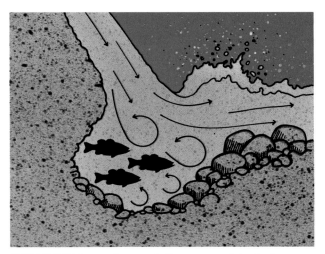

DUGOUTS beneath waterfalls are surprisingly deep. The eddying action of the water undercuts the base of the falls, providing fish an ideal hiding spot.

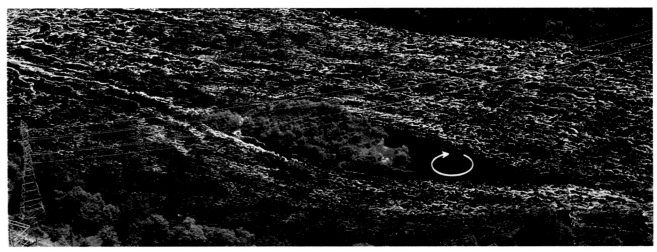

ISLANDS usually have large eddies at the downstream ends, and depending upon their shape, may have smaller eddies at the upstream ends. If the sides are irregular, eddies may form there as well.

Important Types of Overhead Cover

FLOATING-LEAF VEGETATION, such as lily pads, grows in slack water. It attracts species such as sunfish, crappies, northern pike and largemouth bass.

UNDERCUT BANKS usually form along outside bends where current erodes away bank materials. The remaining overhang offers shelter to a variety of gamefish.

DOCKS provide overhead protection and, if the posts are large enough, eddies where fish can escape the current. With an ordinary dock, the planking produces some shade, but a dock with a large canopy offers a considerably larger shaded area.

FRESHLY FALLEN TREES have lots of fine branches to break the current, creating a large eddy that will hold slow-water fish, such as crappies. After a year or two, the small branches rot away, but the tree will still hold current-tolerant species.

SPRING-FED TRIBUTARIES and other springwater sources help keep streams cool enough for fish such as walleyes and northern pike. Without adequate springflow, a stream could support only fish capable of tolerating extremely high water temperatures, such as sunfish and catfish. The only exceptions are streams located in the North or at high altitudes, where summertime water temperatures are moderate.

Water Temperature

What species of fish live in a river or stream depends to a great extent on water temperature. Most anglers realize that trout need cold water and that largemouth bass prefer warmer water, but many do not know that there are considerable differences in temperature preferences even among warmwater fish. The chart below shows the preferred temperature ranges of common warmwater species. Notice that the scale covers a range of more than 30 degrees.

Although most warmwater fish can survive over a much wider range of temperatures than coldwater fish, the temperature range in which they thrive is surprisingly narrow. A warmwater fish could survive in a cold trout stream, but the water temperature would be too low for optimal feeding and growth. So they would find it hard to compete with the trout.

The temperature of a stream depends mainly on the source of its water. To support a diverse fish population, some springflow is usually necessary. With good springflow, the water not only stays cooler in summer, it stays warmer in winter. As a result, fish continue to feed through the winter instead of going dormant in near-freezing water.

Besides the water source, other factors that affect stream temperature include the amount of shade along the streamcourse, the shape of the channel, and the gradient of the streambed.

A heavily shaded stream runs 5 to 10 degrees cooler than a similar stream that lacks shade. Even on the same stream, a shaded reach runs several degrees cooler than a reach completely exposed to sunlight.

A stream with a steep gradient warms more slowly than one with a gradually sloping streambed, all other considerations being equal. Because the water moves much faster in a high-gradient stream, it has less time to absorb heat from the air.

Water in a narrow, deep channel tends to stay cooler than water in a wide, shallow channel because less water comes in contact with the air.

Some streams have one or more lakes along their course. Whether a lake is natural or results from a dam, the stream temperature below the lake will be several degrees warmer than the temperature above it, unless the dam has a coldwater draw (p. 21).

Unlike lakes, streams seldom stratify into temperature layers. Turbulence keeps the water completely mixed. Only in flowing water more than 50 feet deep is there likely to be a significant temperature difference between the surface water and that just above the streambed.

Preferred Temperature Ranges of Warmwater Gamefish*

SPECIES	TEMPERATURE RANGE	SPECIES	TEMPERATURE RANGE
Redbreast sunfish	80° to 84° F	Smallmouth bass	67° to 71° F
Flathead catfish	78° to 82° F	Striped bass	65° to 75° F
Blue catfish	77° to 82° F	White bass	65° to 75° F
Channel catfish	75° to 80° F	Walleye	65° to 75° F
Bluegill	75° to 80° F	Northern pike (under 7 lbs.)	65° to 70° F
Spotted bass	73° to 77° F	Northern pike (over 7 lbs.)	50° to 55° F
Redear sunfish	73° to 77° F	White sturgeon	65° to 70° F
Black, white crappies	70° to 75° F	Wiper	64° to 66° F
Largemouth bass	68° to 78° F	Sauger	62° to 72° F
Muskie	67° to 72° F	Shad	60° to 65° F

*Walleyes, saugers, northern pike and muskies are sometimes called "coolwater" species.

Stream Temperature Changes

Understanding stream temperature changes can make a big difference in your fishing success. In early spring, for instance, most fish species are looking for warm water. If you find a pocket of water a few degrees warmer than the surrounding water, you can enjoy some spectacular fishing. In midsummer, cooler water is often the key.

Shown on these pages is a hypothetical stream with most of the common features that influence water temperature. Many of these features will be found on streams that you fish and will affect water temperature in much the same way.

Water temperatures are color-coded as follows:
■ = Cool
■ = Medium
□ = Warm

NARROW, SHADED portions of a stream warm slowly because little water is exposed to direct sunlight.

STEEP, fast-flowing stream sections warm slowly because the moving water absorbs little heat.

CURRENT

FLAT portions of a stream warm rapidly because the slow-moving water has more time to gain heat.

SURFACE-DRAW dams increase stream temperature by spreading out the water and slowing its flow.

20

SPRINGS reduce the temperature of a stream in a small area below the point of entry.

WIDE, UNSHADED stream sections warm rapidly because much of the water is exposed to the sun.

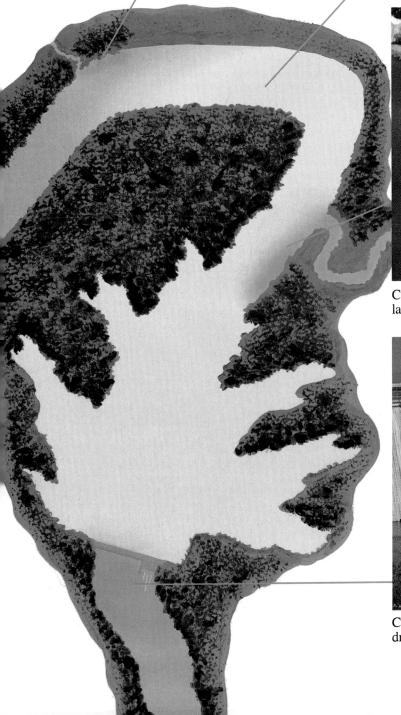

COLDWATER TRIBUTARIES cool the stream over a large area below the point of entry.

COLDWATER DRAWS reduce stream temperature by draining water from the depths of an upstream lake.

Food

Stream fish are opportunists, feeding on whatever food is in greatest supply at the moment. On a windy day, for instance, smallmouth bass may feed heavily on grasshoppers. The bass simply lie along the bank and wait for the morsels to be served.

But stream fish cannot rely solely on food from outside the stream, because the supply is unpredictable and usually seasonal. To support a healthy fish population, the stream itself must be capable of producing ample food in the form of aquatic insects, crustaceans, and baitfish.

Water fertility has a big influence on how much food a stream can produce, and thus the number and size of fish it can support. Just as in a lake, water with a high concentration of dissolved minerals produces more pounds of fish per acre than water with a low level (see below).

A bottom of rocks, gravel or a mixture of the two makes good habitat for aquatic invertebrates and minnows; they can find cover under the rocks and gravel or in the spaces between them. When the bottom silts over, the spaces disappear and many of the food organisms disappear with them. A firm muck bottom will produce some food, mainly the larvae of burrowing insects, such as mayflies. But a clean, sandy bottom produces practically no food. The sand tends to shift with the current, so it provides no cover for invertebrates or anything else.

A stable flow is also important. If the stream is subject to extremely low flows, gravel beds may dry up or freeze solid in winter, killing any food organisms present. When the water comes back up, the stream looks as if everything is normal, but there is little food. Streams of this type cannot support healthy gamefish populations.

Requirements for Good Food Production

FERTILE WATER contains an abundance of plankton, the basic link in the aquatic food chain. Young gamefish feed directly on plankton; older ones on insects and other organisms that eat the plankton.

A ROCKY BOTTOM means a wide variety of gamefish foods, such as aquatic insect larvae, crustaceans and baitfish. Rocks make much better habitat for these small organisms than silt, sand or muck.

How Streams Change

If you have ever returned to fish a stream after several years, you were probably surprised to find that the stream was much different from what you remembered.

The cutting force of moving water keeps all natural streams in a state of flux. New holes are excavated, and new sandbars formed.

Erosion causes bends to move slowly downstream. As water washes against the bank, soil at the downstream end of an outside bend is washed away. The looser the soil and faster the current, the faster the movement.

Even waterfalls may move. As water spills over the falls, erosion at the base undercuts the crest, which then collapses, causing the falls to creep upstream. In some cases, the crest erodes more quickly than the base, eventually converting the falls into a series of rapids.

A severe flood may change the course of a stream altogether. Floodwaters may cut across a major bend, rather than flow around it. The bend, now separated from the stream, becomes an *oxbow lake* (below left).

Floods also carry in logs, brush and other debris that can hang up in shallow or narrow spots, forming logjams. Some logjams block so much of the flow that the stream is forced to make a new channel on one side or the other. Where the logjam slows the current, silt is deposited, eventually forming a new island.

On small, low-gradient streams, beavers can cause major changes. A large beaver dam can back up water for hundreds of yards, creating a fair-sized lake. With the slower current, silt settles out, filling in the streambed. As the stream becomes shallower and wider, it warms more quickly. The water temperature may increase by 10 degrees or more, making the stream unsuitable for many species of fish.

Streams with *braided channels* (below right) change the most. Their bottoms are constantly shifting, and even a minor flood can cut many new channels and fill in old ones.

OXBOW LAKES form when a stream cuts across a neck of land rather than following its channel. The result is a narrow, horseshoe-shaped lake completely separated from the main channel.

BRAIDED CHANNELS are common in streams that flow over loose materials. Instead of one channel, there are two or more, each acting independently. The channels usually cross upstream and downstream of islands.

CHANNEL CHANGES can be easily seen in this high-altitude photo. The present river channel is shown in blue; an old channel in red. The photo also shows many other channel changes that have occurred over the years.

LOOK for fish away from the main channel when a river is at flood stage. The current is lighter there, and the submerged trees and brush provide good cover. Sometimes you'll find the fish in only a foot or two of water.

Tips for Fishing in Rising Water

MOVE upstream if the water is too muddy for good fishing. Often, a single large tributary carries in most of the muddy water. Once you get above the tributary, water clarity improves dramatically.

FLOATING DEBRIS means that the water is rising. As water moves farther up on the banks, logs and brush begin to float away. Streamside grasses and brush are flooded and there is no visible high-water line.

Fluctuating Water Levels

Within a matter of hours after a heavy rain, the level of a stream may rise 10 feet, the current speed may triple, and the normally clear water may turn chocolate brown.

Physical changes of this magnitude make life difficult for the stream fisherman. The fish take up different positions in the stream to avoid the fast and often muddy water.

As the water rises, fish tend to move shallower. And the shallowest water available is usually near the advancing waterline, often right against the bank. There, the water is slower and clearer, and baitfish and insects are more plentiful than in midstream.

When the water starts to drop even the slightest bit, fish move deeper, into deep holes and along steep banks and drop-offs. All types of fish, including baitfish, move out of the shallows. If stream fish did not possess this acute sense for changing water levels, they could be trapped in isolated pools when the water recedes.

Because stream fish respond to even minor changes in water level, experienced stream fishermen pay close attention to water gauges on bridges and dams. They also monitor water-level changes on in-stream objects, such as rocks and logs.

Pay close attention to water clarity following a heavy rain. Clouds of mud rolling downstream usually mean poor fishing because the fish cannot see your bait. If you must fish when the water is high and muddy, work areas close to the bank, where the water is usually clearer.

When the water starts to clear, the fish start to feed heavily and fishing improves. How long it takes for the stream to return to normal depends mainly on the size of its drainage area. The larger the drainage area, the longer it takes.

Small streams fed primarily by springflow cloud up very little and are a good choice when other streams in the area are too muddy. The springflow also maintains the water level during a drought.

Tips for Fishing in Falling Water

CHECK a water gauge to determine when the water level is starting to drop. It's important to monitor the level closely; a drop of only an inch or two may cause gamefish to abandon the shallows.

SILT freshly deposited on streamside weeds, trees or rocks means that the water is falling and fish are moving deeper. When the water level is dropping, the stream carries little floating debris.

CROSS behind a barge or ship to reach the other side of the river. If you're ahead of the vessel, circle behind or wait for it to pass. If you cross in front, the vessel may not be able to stop in time should your motor kill.

River Navigation

Anyone who fishes navigable rivers should be familiar with "the rules of the road." What is the procedure for passing other boats? What do the buoys, signs and signals mean? How do I pass through a lock? What hazards should I watch for?

While these questions are obviously important, many anglers, even those with years of river-fishing experience, do not understand the basics of river navigation. And many have suffered serious accidents as a result of their ignorance.

RULES OF THE ROAD. When approaching another boat head-on, steer to the right to avoid a collision. However, if two boats are far enough to the left of each other, no course alteration is needed.

When another boat moving the same direction attempts to pass you, maintain your course and speed. When you pass another boat, keep enough distance so your wake does not endanger the other boat.

If two boats approach each other at a right angle, the boat to the right has the right-of-way. Canoes and other nonmotorized boats have the right-of-way over motorized boats, except when the nonmotorized boat is overtaking or passing.

Always yield the right-of-way to an emergency craft displaying a red or blue flashing light.

MOORING BUOYS, when upright, have a blue horizontal stripe on a white background.

CHANNEL MARKERS designate the edges of the navigation channel. When heading upstream, you'll see red buoys on the right; green on the left. Remember the three Rs: red-right-return.

MILE MARKERS are found along the navigation channel of major rivers. Signs along the Mississippi River, for instance, give distance in miles above the mouth of the Ohio River.

OTHER NAVIGATION BUOYS warn you of hazards, give regulations or provide information. A buoy with (1) red and white vertical stripes means you should not pass on the side toward shore. A (2) white buoy with an orange diamond means a hazard, such as a boulder. A (3) white buoy with an orange circle means a restricted area, such as a no-wake zone. A (4) white buoy with an orange square gives boating information or directions.

LOCK-THROUGH PROCEDURES.

Before entering a lock, look for signs that give you instructions. In most cases, there is a pull rope about 1,000 feet from the lock. When you pull, a bell notifies the lockmaster that you wish to lock through.

Pull rope and wait for signal to change

Enter lock on green light

Normally a red signal light on the lock flashes while the lock is being prepared for entry. When the lock is ready, the signal changes to green, meaning you should motor slowly into the lock.

When you're inside the lock, the gates will close and the water will rise or fall, depending on which direction you're heading. The attendant may throw you a rope to keep your boat from drifting, but never tie this rope to your boat. When the water drops, the rope could tighten, keeping your boat from dropping with the water.

To exit the lock, wait for the gates to open and the red signal inside the lock to turn green, then motor out slowly.

HAZARDS. One of the most common river hazards is a submerged deadhead. Water-soaked logs often drift just beneath the surface or barely protrude from it. If you hit a deadhead at high speed, you could seriously damage or even capsize your boat.

Watch for deadheads

Deadheads are most common when the water is rising. As the river swells, logs and other objects on shore float away. Under these conditions, boaters should reduce their speed and watch carefully for any surface disturbance.

Boaters that approach a dam too closely, especially in high water, risk getting sucked into the heavy current. Strong eddies below the dam create turbulence that can trap a boat and even suck it under. The best advice is to stay away from the fast water below a dam.

Don't motor this close to a dam

Slow down for the wake of a barge

Always be on the lookout for wakes from barges, ships, houseboats and cruisers. Instead of crashing through the wake with a small boat, slow down and ride it out like a cork. If you hit a large wake at high speed, your bow could plow under the water.

When fishing in the main channel, be alert for barges or other large boats that could slip up on you with no warning. On a windy day, you may not hear the sound of the engines in time to get your motor started.

Look out for wing dams

Submerged wing dams are the nemesis of boaters who venture out of the main channel. Often, the rock structures are less than a foot beneath the surface, just the right depth to damage a propeller or even shear off a lower unit. Look for a line of ripples and a slight dip in the surface at a right angle to the direction of flow.

Anchoring in fast current is not a good idea, but if you must anchor, attach your rope to the bow eye, not to the gunwale or stern. If you anchor sideways, the current could flip your boat. If you anchor from the stern, the current could push water up and over the transom.

International Scale of River Difficulty

Before attempting to navigate any river, be sure you know the degree of difficulty of its rapids. To standardize the terminology used in describing rapids, the International Scale of River Difficulty was developed.

The difficulty level of a rapids may vary, depending on the water stage. For instance, high water can turn a class 2 rapids into a class 3 or 4. If you're unsure of the difficulty level or have trouble seeing the rapids, land your boat and scout from shore before attempting to run it.

Following are descriptions of the six grades of white-water difficulty:

CLASS 1. Easy rapids with small standing waves and few obstructions. May disappear in high water.

CLASS 2. Standing waves may reach a height of 3 feet. Some maneuvering is required for safe passage. As a rule, anglers in small fishing boats should avoid any rapids greater than class 2.

CLASS 3. High, irregular standing waves are capable of swamping an open canoe or small boat. Extensive maneuvering may be required to follow narrow chutes between boulders or turbulent areas.

CLASS 4. High, irregular standing waves, constricted passages and blind drops require a rubber raft, decked canoe, kayak or maneuverable deep-sided boat, such as a McKenzie River boat or jet boat.

CLASS 5. Hazardous to life because of long, violent rapids and steep drops or falls, which may require a complex route to navigate. Runnable only by experts with a raft or fully decked boat.

CLASS 6. Same hazards as class 5 rapids, but more severe. Even whitewater experts consider class 6 rapids nearly impossible to navigate. These torrents pose a great risk to life.

Fishing Rivers & Streams

Midwestern Mainstem Rivers

*When fishing a mainstem river,
you'll always catch something,
but you're never sure what it will be*

Because of the tremendous importance of river transportation in the 1800s, most large midwestern cities developed along the banks of major waterways. Today, millions of anglers live within easy driving distance of these rivers.

A *mainstem* river could be defined as the major river into which all other rivers and streams in a given drainage system flow. As a rule, these rivers share the following characteristics:

- large size, usually 10,000 cubic feet per second or more.

- murky water, especially if located in farm country.

- pattern of severe flooding and dramatic changes in water level.

- dams along their course, to control floods and maintain water levels for navigation.

- a diverse fish population; fish can move into the river from a large tributary network.

Many of these rivers are still important navigation routes, accommodating barges carrying commodities such as grain, coal and oil. As such, the rivers are often subject to dredging, channelization and pollution. In some, the gamefish population has dwindled to the point where there is very little sport fishing.

But big rivers are remarkably resilient; despite man's disregard for these mainstem waterways, many still provide excellent multispecies fishing. Some support a dozen or more gamefish species and even more species of roughfish.

Mississippi River, Minnesota and Wisconsin

THE UPPER MISSISSIPPI has a complex network of backwater lakes, sloughs and connecting channels.

Case Study:

Upper Mississippi River, Minnesota & Wisconsin

One of the best examples of a midwestern mainstem river is the Upper Mississippi where it splits the states of Minnesota and Wisconsin. The 118-mile stretch from Lock and Dam No. 3 upstream of Red Wing, Minnesota, to Lock and Dam No. 8 near Genoa, Wisconsin, is regarded as the river's most varied and productive zone.

When the U.S. Army Corps of Engineers built these dams in the 1930s, thousands of acres of marshland

Because of the diverse habitat, this portion of the river supports a variety of gamefish and roughfish.

adjacent to the river were flooded, creating a maze of backwater lakes connected to the main river by narrow cuts.

"Ol' Man River isn't really a river at all," wrote Mel Ellis in the *Milwaukee Journal* in 1949. "In fact, he's a hundred rivers and a thousand lakes and more sloughs than you could explore in a lifetime."

The navigation channel in this stretch averages 300 feet wide and 12 feet deep, although there are holes more than 30 feet deep. Along the channel is the *main-channel border,* a shallower zone extending from the edge of the channel to shore. In this area are numerous wing dams, structures made of rocks and sticks that deflect the current toward the center of the river. Constructed in the late 1800s and early 1900s, the wing dams help keep the channel from filling in with sand.

Current speed in the main channel measures 1 to 2 mph at normal water stage; up to 6 in high water. Current-tolerant species, such as smallmouth bass, white bass, catfish, walleye, sauger and sturgeon,

THE LOWER MISSISSIPPI, from Alton, Illinois, downstream, has little habitat diversity because the river is confined between high banks or levees. Roughfish predominate, with few gamefish species present.

spend most of their time in the main channel or along the main-channel border. Man-made cover is very important in this zone. Besides wing dams, man-made cover includes riprapped shorelines, bridge pilings, and the rock piles that support channel markers.

Navigation dams are spaced at 10- to 44-mile intervals along the Upper Mississippi River. Each has a lock to allow passage of boats, including river barges. The dams are not high compared to dams on most other major rivers. They hold back only 6 to 9 feet of water at normal stage. Most of the dams are too low to create a lakelike zone upstream, although the river above a dam is nonetheless called a pool. Each dam has a number, and the pool extending upstream to the next dam has the same number. For example, Pool 5 encompasses all of the water area from Lock and Dam No. 5 upstream to Lock and Dam No. 4.

The dams provide good habitat for many kinds of gamefish, especially the current-tolerant species. The large eddies that form below the gates and along the edges of the fast-water zone provide refuge from the swift current.

Backwaters generally have little or no current, average less than 5 feet deep, and have excellent cover, including flooded trees and stumps, and lush stands of submerged and emergent vegetation. They make ideal habitat for slack-water species such as largemouth bass, northern pike, sunfish and crappies. Other species, such as smallmouth bass and catfish, use the backwaters for spawning.

Although backwaters may be found anywhere in a pool, the most extensive ones are usually at a pool's lower end, where the dam elevates water levels the most.

Some of the backwater areas are vast, covering several thousand acres. In these areas, the river (including the main channel and backwaters) may be more than 3 miles wide.

Another type of habitat found in the Upper Mississippi is a *river lake*. The best example is Lake Pepin,

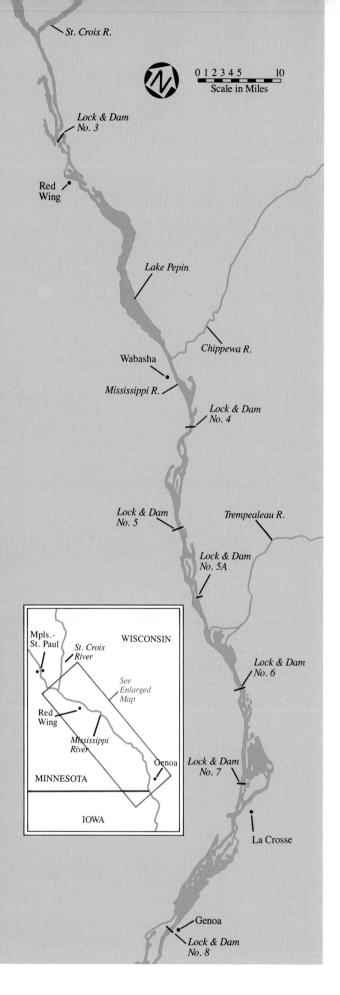

YOUNG-OF-THE-YEAR SHAD (top) are ideal for food. They predominate because of the annual die-off. If not for the die-off, there would be more older shad (bottom), too large for food, and fewer young ones.

a 25,000-acre body of water formed by the delta of the Chippewa River. The delta acts somewhat like a dam, partially blocking the flow of the Mississippi and creating a lakelike environment upstream. The lake has very little current, except at the extreme upper and lower ends. The average depth is about 20 feet; the maximum, 65. Lake Pepin holds good populations of practically all gamefish found in the river.

One of the biggest challenges in fishing a big river, especially one with such diverse habitat, is locating fish at different water stages. Runoff generally peaks in mid- to late April, and the water level may rise as much as 20 feet above normal. As the water rises, fish abandon their normal haunts. They continue moving until the water level returns to normal. Rainy weather in summer and fall may cause the river to rise several feet, enough to move gamefish out of their usual habitat. But

High-water mark

these movements are seldom as dramatic as those associated with spring runoff.

The primary food for most of the river's gamefish is the gizzard shad, a species found in few other waters in the region. This portion of the river is at the northern edge of the shad's range, so most of the annual crop dies off in winter because of the cold water. But some shad survive the winter by staying in spring holes and warmwater discharges

GAMEFISH in the Upper Mississippi grow rapidly because of the abundant food supply. The highly fertile water teems with plankton that nourishes invertebrates and baitfish. The Mississippi's fast-growing gamefish have smaller heads and fatter bodies than fish from most other waters in the region. Notice the difference in body shape between a Mississippi River walleye and a slower-growing walleye (inset) from a nearby lake.

from power plants. At first glance, the shad die-off would seem counterproductive to good fish production. But the reverse is actually true (see opposite page).

Most of the fishing on the Upper Mississippi is done from small boats, although there is a great

Fishing barge

deal of bank fishing and some fishing from commercially operated barges moored in the tailwaters of several of the dams. For a small daily fee, barge operators will ferry you out to fish from a floating platform anchored in a prime fishing area.

Jon boats and semi-V aluminum boats from 14 to 16 feet are popular in this area. Because they draw very little water, they can run cuts and sloughs where larger boats would bottom out.

One of the major environmental problems on the river is dredging. The main channel must be dredged frequently by the Corps of Engineers to maintain the minimum 9-foot channel depth necessary for barge traffic. The dredge spoil (10 percent sand,

Spoil from dredging operation

90 percent water) is pumped onto land adjacent to the river, often spilling into backwater lakes and sloughs and channels leading into the backwaters. The sand smothers bottom organisms and plant life, greatly reducing the backwaters' capacity to produce gamefish.

The fishing season for most gamefish is open year around on this part of the Mississippi. Prime fishing times for each species vary considerably, but you can bet that something will be biting every month of the year.

Upper Mississippi River Physical Data (at Wabasha)	
Average width	1,000 ft
Average depth	12 ft
Gradient	low
Clarity	1.5 ft
Color	brown
Discharge (cubic feet per second)	33,300
Winter low temperature	32° F
Summer high temperature	85° F

43

MAIN CHANNEL is home to a variety of gamefish, mainly walleyes, saugers, smallmouths, white bass and catfish.

RIPRAP shorelines provide better cover than sand or muck. They attract practically all species of gamefish.

WING DAMS deflect water toward the center of the river. They're best for smallmouths and walleyes.

CLOSING DAMS were built to restrict the flow into back-waters, keeping more water in the main channel. The rocky structures attract smallmouths and walleyes.

RUNNING SLOUGHS have a major inlet and outlet, so there is a noticeable current. They are well suited to smallmouth bass, catfish and, in spring, walleyes.

SIDE CHANNELS connect backwater lakes and sloughs to the main channel. They make good habitat for largemouth and smallmouth bass, walleyes and catfish.

BACKWATER LAKES are deeper and have less submerged vegetation than dead sloughs, but hold the same fish.

DEAD SLOUGHS have no outlet, so the water is slack. They hold largemouths, panfish and pike.

TAILWATERS are known for spring walleye and sauger fishing, but draw most river gamefish some time of year.

SAUGERS (left) and walleyes (right) are easy to tell apart. Saugers have prominent black spots on the dorsal fin. Walleyes lack the spots, but the dorsal has a dark blotch at the lower rear.

Upper Mississippi River:
Walleyes & Saugers

Each spring, Mississippi River walleye and sauger fishing makes the news as anglers record spectacular catches below the dams. When the spring spawning run is over, fishing interest shifts to the lakes, and the river is all but forgotten. But those who fish the river regularly enjoy good walleye and sauger action throughout the season.

In the Upper Mississippi, as in most other midwestern mainstem rivers, saugers outnumber walleyes by a wide margin. They are better adapted to turbid, moving water. Walleyes are considerably larger, however; they run 2 to 3 pounds and reach weights over 14. Saugers run 1 to 2 and occasionally reach 6. In 1988, the river produced the Minnesota record sauger, 6 pounds, 2¾ ounces.

Starting as early as mid-September, walleyes and saugers begin moving upstream toward the tailwater areas, where they will spawn the next spring.

They feed sporadically through the winter, mostly in water from 15 to 25 feet deep. Anglers catch them by vertically jigging in the tailwaters, working the edges of the fast water with ¼- to ⅜-ounce chartreuse jigs tipped with minnows. The fish, particularly the saugers, tend to strike short in the cold water, so you may have to add a stinger hook to your jig.

As spawning time approaches and the water warms into the 40s, the fish move shallower and begin feeding much more heavily. The two-week period before spawning offers the fastest action and the best opportunity for big fish.

Big walleyes congregate in eddies near the rock or gravel shorelines where they will spawn, usually at depths of 2 to 8 feet. Many walleye anglers make the mistake of fishing too deep in this pre-spawn period. Saugers stay 5 to 10 feet deeper than the walleyes.

If the water is high, as it often is this time of year, walleyes leave the main channel and move to the backwaters, where finding them is next to impossible. Saugers are less likely to leave the main channel.

You can catch walleyes by anchoring and casting into shallow brushy or riprapped shorelines with

BRUSHY SHORELINES with rock or gravel bottoms draw big walleyes at spawning time. Most anglers avoid these areas for fear of getting snagged, but you can easily fish the edges of the brush or pockets in it.

How to Jig-Troll for Walleyes and Saugers

FLIP a ⅛- to ¼-ounce jig a short distance from the boat, keeping the bail open as the jig sinks. Or simply lower the jig vertically until it hits bottom.

BACKTROLL slowly with an electric motor while jigging. Always troll with the current; if you troll against the current, you'll have trouble reaching bottom.

KEEP your line as close to vertical as you can while twitching the jig, then lowering it to the bottom. If you let out too much line, the jig will drag along the bottom with no action. Set the hook when you feel a tap.

white or chartreuse jigs, from ⅛ to ¼ ounce. Saugers are best taken by vertically jigging in deeper water with ¼- to ⅜-ounce jigs. Some anglers prefer to tip their jigs with small minnows, but tipping is seldom necessary when the water temperature tops 40° F. For best results, work the jig very slowly, with small hops.

Spawning begins when the water reaches the upper 40s, usually in mid- to late April. Saugers start to spawn a few days later than walleyes. Once spawning is under way, fishing turns sour. You may catch a few small males, but the big females don't start to bite until at least two weeks after they've finished spawning.

Starting about the first week in May, big walleyes go on a feeding spree that produces plenty of trophy fish for fishermen who know where to find them. Most of the fish have moved away from the dam, although a few remain all summer. The best spots are backwaters with moving water and current-brushed points in the main channel several miles downstream from the dam. You'll find most of the fish at depths of 8 to 12 feet. Productive techniques include anchoring above the points and casting with ¼-ounce chartreuse bucktail jigs, or trolling diving plugs through channels in the backwaters.

Saugers are not far away, although they normally hang at least 5 feet deeper than the walleyes.

Over the next few weeks, the fish scatter throughout the pool. As the water drops, most of them abandon the backwaters and take up residence in the main channel, usually near wing dams or along riprapped shoreline. Some hold in eddies in cuts leading into the backwaters. Typical summertime

LURES AND RIGS for walleyes and saugers include: (1) Fire-Ball Jig and minnow, with the removable stinger hook clipped to the rear eye of the jig, and one prong of the treble hook inserted into the minnow; (2) ¼-ounce Mister

depths for walleyes are 10 to 15 feet; for saugers, 15 to 25 feet. The fish stay in these areas into September, then start working their way back toward the dam.

In summer and fall, most anglers fish with chartreuse or green bucktail or twister-tail jigs, from ¼ to ⅜ ounce. Effective jig-fishing techniques include jigging vertically while drifting with the current, anchoring and casting in an eddy or above a wing dam, or jig-trolling (opposite page). Slip-sinker rigs baited with nightcrawlers also work well. Simply lower the rig to the bottom and drift with the current, keeping your line as vertical as possible. Another productive walleye-sauger bait is the willow cat, or madtom, a small, bullheadlike fish found in weedy sloughs.

One of the oldest walleye-sauger techniques on the river is trolling with lead-core line. Anglers use short, stiff trolling rods and level-wind reels spooled with 25- to 40-pound lead core. A crankbait, minnow plug or vibrating plug is attached to a 3-foot leader of 10- to 14-pound mono. The plug is trolled upstream along the edge of the channel or along any lengthy drop-off. The lead-core line makes it easy to get the plug down in the current. Lead-core trolling may not be the most sporting method, but it's certainly among the most effective.

A 5½- to 6-foot spinning outfit with 6- to 8-pound mono is adequate for most other walleye and sauger fishing. Select a fast-action rod for jigging and trolling; a medium action for live-bait fishing.

Because of the murky water, walleyes and saugers in the Mississippi generally bite best in sunny weather, and midday is often more productive than morning or evening.

How to Lead-Line for Walleyes and Saugers

TROLL upstream when lead-lining. Water resistance gives the plug its action; if you troll downstream, water resistance is much less.

LET OUT enough line to reach bottom. Because the line is color coded, you'll soon learn exactly how much line to let out to reach a certain depth.

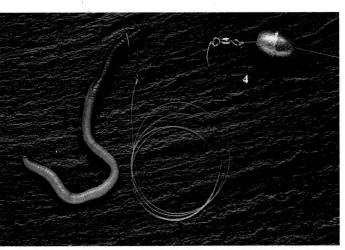

Twister Meeny Jig; (3) Mirrolure; (4) slip-sinker rig tied with a 2- to 3-foot leader of 6-pound mono, a ⅜- to ½-ounce egg sinker, and a size 4 hook baited with a nightcrawler.

REEL IN a few turns when you feel the plug bumping bottom; let out more line if you haven't felt it bump for a while. Continue to adjust your depth as you troll along. When a fish strikes, it usually hooks itself.

49

Upper Mississippi River:
Bluegills & Crappies

Bull 'gills and slab crappies abound in the Upper Mississippi. Not that you'll find them everywhere, but if you know where to look, you can catch bluegills weighing a pound or more, and crappies pushing 2. The Minnesota record black crappie, 5 pounds, was caught in the Vermillion River a short distance from where it empties into the Mississippi.

Catching bluegills and crappies is easiest in spring, when they're schooled up near their spawning beds. The trick is finding the beds.

Crappies move into their spawning areas a little earlier than bluegills. Crappies spawn at water temperatures in the low to mid-60s; bluegills in the mid- to upper 60s.

Both species spawn in shallow backwater areas, usually along gradually sloping banks with a sand-gravel bottom. The best backwaters are those with a good growth of submerged vegetation. As a rule, you can find the fish around brush piles, tree roots or newly developing weeds in water less than 3 feet deep.

Most anglers prefer live bait, small minnows for crappies; worms, small leeches or waxworms for bluegills. Simply attach a small float and dangle the bait in openings in the brush or weeds. Both species will hit small white or yellow twister- or

How to Fish Pockets in the Brush

FLIP a bobber rig by stripping line off your reel with one hand, and then with an underhand flippin' motion similar to that used in bass fishing, guide the rig into pockets in the brush.

LURES AND RIGS include: bobber rig with (1) leech, (2) worm, (3) waxworm, and (4) minnow (crappies only); (5) Midget and waxworm; (6) squid-tail jig; (7) Jigging Rapala (crappies only); (8) Lightning Bug (sunfish only).

SET the hook immediately when the float goes under, then quickly hoist the fish vertically from the water. If you wait too long to set the hook or let the fish run too far, it will tangle your line in the brush.

squid-tail jigs from 1/32 to 1/16 ounce. Small yellow fly-rod poppers also work well for bluegills.

After the spawning period, the fish scatter throughout the backwaters and some even move into the main channel. Prime backwater locations include fallen trees, cane beds, and flats with scattered submerged vegetation.

Crappies will tolerate more current than bluegills. In the main channel or in Lake Pepin, look for them along deep riprapped banks brushed by light current or along rocky piers. Some even move into the tailwaters, schooling in deep eddies along the edges of the fast water. Bluegills can be found in shallower water along riprapped banks where the water is nearly slack. They also hang on weedy wing dams with very slow current.

A light spinning outfit, about 5 feet long, spooled with 4-pound mono works well for bobber fishing in open cover or casting tiny jigs. But when you're fishing pockets in fallen trees or cane beds, a long extension pole or cane pole is a better choice. Rig your bait so it hangs a few feet beneath a small float. Then use the long pole to swing the rig in and out of tight pockets in the cover.

Crappies usually bite best early or late in the day. Bluegills start biting later and quit earlier, although there is often a spurt of fast action just before sunset. Overcast weather is best for crappies; sunny weather for bluegills.

As the water cools in fall, bluegills and crappies congregate in slack portions of the backwaters. Anglers who venture out on thin ice enjoy some of the year's fastest fishing, sometimes in water less than 3 feet deep. But if you're not familiar with the area, don't leave the beaten track. The ice thickness varies tremendously because of unpredictable currents.

Teardrops tipped with waxworms account for most of the bluegills. This bait also takes its share of crappies, but a small minnow beneath a tiny float or a jigging Rapala may work better. The action slows in midwinter as the fish move deeper. Some bluegills and crappies continue to be caught at depths of 10 feet or less, but in backwater lakes with deep holes, crappies may suspend over water 20 to 30 feet deep. The action picks up again as the ice starts to melt in March and the fish move back to shallower water.

CAST a slip-bobber rig into open water alongside a rocky pier or steep, riprapped shoreline. Crappies suspend in these areas, usually about 10 feet down, and are difficult to reach with other methods. You can also cast out a 1/16-ounce jig, then count it down to the right depth, but a slip-bobber offers better depth control.

Tips for Catching Sunfish and Crappies

WORK the inside edge of the weeds to catch sunfish at spawning time. Often there is a band of clean bottom near shore where winter ice prevents weeds from taking root.

CAST a light jig into a rocky shoreline and bounce it down the break to catch crappies. When a fish strikes, note the depth, then cast parallel to shore at that depth.

FISH any cuts or openings between weedbeds to catch sunfish. They're more likely to be in the openings than in the thick weeds, and the openings are easier to work.

USE a cane pole or extension pole to reach pockets in tall weeds, such as cane. The long pole also enables you to lift fish out vertically so they don't tangle in weeds.

Upper Mississippi River:
Largemouth Bass

The Mississippi's weedy, stump-strewn backwaters are made-to-order for largemouth bass. The fish start to bite in late April, when the water warms to about 55° F. In early season, the warmest water generally holds the most bass.

From late April through May, you'll find bass in beds of green weeds around stumps close to deep water. Work the weeds using spinnerbaits, or run a bright-colored crankbait over the weedtops. For fishing pockets in thick beds of coontail or lily pads, try flippin' with a jig-and-pig. A slower-than-normal retrieve works best in spring.

Weedy backwaters produce bass throughout the summer, but some of the fish move into the main channel and side channels, where there is more current. When changes in weather, such as cold fronts, cause fishing in the backwaters to slow, bass in these channels continue to bite. The fish are not actually in the current but hold in eddies near current.

Prime channel areas include deep eddies near the head of an island, and wing dams with slow-moving water. You'll also find bass on sand flats near deep water, around beaver houses, along riprapped shorelines or islands, and in eddies created by bridge pilings. Few weeds grow in these areas, so most of the bass hang near timber.

Work the timber by flippin' a jig-and-pig or casting a crankbait into an opening, then bumping the wood as you retrieve. Plastic worms and spinnerbaits also account for a lot of bass. When fishing early or late in the day or during a light rain, try retrieving a buzzbait tight to the cover.

In July and August, largemouths may follow schools of surface-feeding shad. You can find the shad by looking for ripples on the surface on a calm day. Select a light-colored lure that you can cast a long way, such as a Sonar, jig or crankbait. Then retrieve it through or just below the shad. Be sure to stay far enough away to avoid spooking the bass.

Bass start to school in September and October. In early fall, you can still catch them in the main channel and side channels, but by mid-September most are moving into the backwaters. Weeds in the backwaters are beginning to die, so bass move into deep holes to find cover and spend the winter. But if you can find green weeds, you'll probably find bass. Another good fall location is a riprapped railroad embankment in the backwaters.

LURES AND RIGS for largemouths include: (1) Bomber Model A, (2) Heddon Sonar, (3) Buzz-ard buzzbait, (4) Lazer Eye spinnerbait, (5) River Rat Ringworm rigged Texas-style using a 2/0 hook and a bullet sinker pegged with a toothpick, (6) Hildebob rubber-skirted jig tipped with a size 11 Uncle Josh pork frog.

When bass are in deep holes or along deep banks, try a crankbait or jig-and-pig. On a warm, sunny day, they may move up on shallow flats next to the deep water, where you can catch them on spinnerbaits. Use larger baits in fall and work them more slowly than in summer. Fishing stays good until the water cools below 50° F.

During the first few weeks after freeze up, ice fishermen catch some largemouths in shallow, weedy backwaters. Most bass are taken by accident by pike anglers using tip-ups baited with big minnows, or panfish anglers jigging teardrops tipped with waxworms.

Largemouths bite best during periods of stable weather, although the action is usually fast just before a front. As a rule, cloudy days are better than sunny ones; mornings and evenings better than midday.

Upper Mississippi largemouths run from 1 to 3 pounds and occasionally reach weights up to 6. They spend a good deal of their time around dense cover, so most anglers use beefy tackle. A medium-heavy 5½- to 6-foot baitcasting outfit with 17-pound mono is a good all-around choice. For pitchin' (below), use a reel with a thumb bar and set the spool tension as loose as possible.

Pitchin' for Largemouths

QUIETLY APPROACH the cover you plan to fish. Stop within 15 to 20 feet of the cover.

POINT the rod tip down so you can cast with an upward motion; hold the lure in your other hand.

PITCH the lure with a low trajectory. To minimize splash, thumb the reel just before the lure hits.

Upper Mississippi River:
Smallmouth Bass

In the early 1900s, the Upper Mississippi was renowned for its smallmouth bass fishing. The fish were big and plentiful. Four- to six-pounders were common, and a few exceeded 7.

The river still produces trophy smallmouths, but today you'll have to work a little harder for them. Most of the fish run 1½ to 2½ pounds.

Beginning in early May, smallmouths move into certain backwater areas where they spawn each year. Like largemouths, they start to bite when the water temperature reaches about 55° F. The best areas are less than 5 feet deep, have firm sand or gravel bottoms with rocks, logs, stumps or brush for cover, and are near but not in current.

The most popular springtime lure is a ⅛- to ¼-ounce jig–plastic grub combo. Other good lures include 4-inch plastic worms; small, shallow-running crankbaits and minnow plugs; and ⅛- to ¼-ounce spinnerbaits. With any of these lures, a slow retrieve works best in spring.

The bass finish spawning by late May, then filter out of the backwaters. Smallmouths everywhere love rocks, and the Mississippi River is no exception. Starting in early June, they start to congregate off rocky points, along riprapped banks and along the upstream lips of main-channel wing dams. The best wing dams have little sand or silt and plenty of exposed rock. Rocky areas in side channels also hold

LURES AND RIGS for smallmouths include: (1) Fuzz-E-Grub, (2) Lightning Bug, (3) River Rat Ringworm, Texas-rigged with a bullet sinker, (4) Mepps Bass Killer, (5) Original Floating Rapala, (6) Shad Rap.

How to Fish a Wing Dam with a Popper

ANCHOR upstream of a wing dam, within easy fly-casting distance of the upper lip. Select a spot where the current is moderate. As a rule, the current gets slower as you move toward shore; faster toward the outside end of the wing dam.

CAST downstream; the popper should alight on top of the wing dam. Twitch the popper so it barely disturbs the surface (inset), pause a few seconds, strip in 1 to 2 feet of line, then give it another twitch. When the popper is about 10 feet above the wing dam, pick up and cast again.

smallmouths, as do sand flats along channel edges. Weedy flats hold more fish than those with clean sand bottoms. Another good spot is an eddy around a bridge piling with a rock pile at its base. As a rule, you'll find the fish at depths of 12 feet or less through the summer.

When smallmouths are rooting crayfish from the rocks, they'll hit deep-diving crankbaits; 1/4- to 3/8-ounce jig-grub or jig-and-pig combos, or tube jigs; and 6-inch Texas-rigged plastic worms. Fly fishermen enjoy fast surface action early or late in the day on divers, poppers and sliders.

You can catch some smallmouths in these rocky areas through the summer and into fall. Most of the bass move shallower in fall, but the biggest ones hang on the deep ends of the wing dams. Fall fishing peaks in late September or early October as the fish start feeding up for winter. They're more

concentrated than in summer, so if you catch one, there's a good chance there will be more. This late-season feeding binge usually starts when the water temperature drops below 60° F. Use the same lures you would in summer. Smallmouths feed very little from late fall through the winter months.

Like largemouths, smallmouths bite best in stable weather, on overcast days, and in morning and evening. But early or late in the season, the action is often fastest in the middle of the day.

Serious smallmouth anglers carry at least two rods: a 5½- to 6-foot medium-power baitcasting outfit with 10- to 14-pound mono for crankbaits, spinner-baits, plastic worms and jig-and-pig combos; and a 5- to 6-foot medium-light spinning outfit with 4- to 6-pound mono, for light jigs and minnow plugs. For fly-fishing, use a 9-foot, 7-weight rod with a floating, weight-forward line.

Northern Pike

Northerns grow big in the Upper Mississippi; it's not unusual to catch limits averaging over 10 pounds, and pike exceeding 25 pounds are caught each season. Pike of this size are unusual in the region's natural lakes, especially in Minnesota, where most lakes are still open to winter pike spearing.

In early spring, the rising water draws pike into shallow backwaters and up small creeks. They swim into the current and will keep going as long as there is enough water to let them pass. During a flood, they may swim into farm fields, miles from the main channel.

As soon as the backwaters are ice free, anglers go after pike with spinnerbaits. The best technique is to move slowly along the shore-line, working the lure in water less than 5 feet deep.

Some pike remain in the back-waters through the summer, the biggest ones seeking out coldwater pockets formed by springs, artesian wells or cold tributaries.

If the cold water flows into the main channel, it is soon swept away and dissipated by the current. But if it flows into a sheltered spot in the backwaters, or into a harbor or bay, it forms a cold layer on the bottom. The layer may be only a foot thick, or it may be 10 feet thick, depending on the size of the source.

These coldwater pockets may be hard to find. In summer you would have to explore by dragging an electric thermometer along the bottom. The pockets are easier to locate in winter because the spring water prevents ice from forming.

Once you find one of these pockets, the rest is easy. Simply dangle a 6- to 10-inch sucker below a good-sized slip-bobber set so the bait is in the coldwater zone. Then wait. If the pike are around, it won't be long. Pike stay in coldwater pockets until late September or, if the weather stays warm, early October.

You can also catch pike by trolling big plugs or casting spoons and bucktails in shallow weedy areas throughout the backwaters, around weedy main-channel wing dams, or along rocky shorelines with slow current. But these fish run smaller than those in the coldwater pockets.

Pike will bite any time of day, although the action slows considerably after the sun goes down. Weather has little effect on pike fishing. They seem to bite out of irritation as much as hunger; a pike will attack a lure when its stomach is stuffed with baitfish.

Big pike require stout tackle. A heavy baitcasting outfit, about 6 feet long, spooled with 15- to 20-pound mono or 20-pound Dacron, is a good all-around choice. A wire leader is a must. A jaw spreader and longnose pliers are recommended for removing hooks.

In late fall, pike concentrate in shallow, weedy backwaters. They stay there through winter. Anglers using tip-ups baited with big minnows catch a surprising number of 10-pound-plus pike, especially in early winter, when the ice is only a few inches thick.

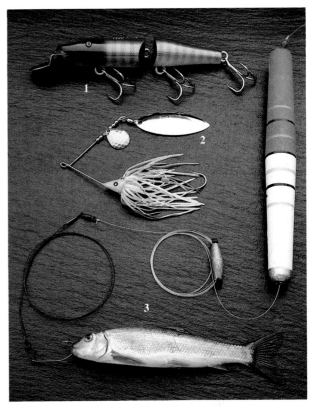

LURES AND RIGS include: (1) Jointed Creek Chub Pikie; (2) Big Bass; (3) slip-bobber rig tied with a cylinder float, Rubber Cor sinker, 20-pound wire leader and a size 2/0 hook. Sucker is hooked through upper lip only.

Where to Find Coldwater Pike

COULEE CREEKS carry in springwater from hills along the river. Although the flow in many of these creeks is very small, they may draw pike if they flow into a sheltered bay or harbor.

SPRING SEEPS that flow directly into the river may be difficult to see, but like coulee creeks, they attract pike if they flow into an area protected from the wind and current.

TROUT STREAMS are prime pike attractors. Large streams have enough cold water to draw pike, even if they flow directly into the main channel. Small streams attract pike only if they flow into a sheltered area.

SPRING HOLES are easiest to find in winter. Spring water stays at the same temperature year around, so in winter, spring holes do not freeze. Note the location of the holes, then try them the following summer.

Upper Mississippi River:
White Bass

For some reason, these scrappy fighters are not as popular in the North as in the South, but it's not for lack of numbers or size. In the Upper Mississippi, it's not uncommon to catch 50 in an hour, most running from 1 to 2½ pounds. The Wisconsin record white bass, 4 pounds, was caught in 1974 on one of the river's commercially operated fishing barges.

White bass spawn in tailwater areas in late April or early May, about two weeks after the walleyes. Huge schools move into eddies below the dams and will bite on small jigs, spinners, plugs or just about anything you throw at them.

After spawning, most of the fish move downriver, stopping to feed in bays and backwater lakes that have warmed more than the main channel and have drawn in schools of shiners and other baitfish.

By early June, the fish have scattered throughout the pool, mainly in the main channel, along the main-channel border, and in cuts flowing into the backwaters. Fishing may be spotty in early summer because the fish are constantly on the move in search of baitfish. A spot where you catch them one day could be dead the next day.

Starting in early September, young-of-the-year gizzard shad begin forming dense schools, which attract the feeding bass. The bass feed in packs, driving the shad to the surface or herding them into bays, then slashing into them in a wild frenzy. You can easily find these feeding schools by watching for gulls screeching and diving into the water to pick up injured shad.

If you spot a flock of diving gulls, get to the area quickly, but don't run your boat into the school, or the fish will spook and may not come up again in the same area. The best strategy is to cut your motor upwind of the school and then drift to within casting distance. An electric motor will help you stay with the school without spooking them.

Once you're in position, cast jigs, tailspins or crankbaits into the melee. The type or color of lure doesn't matter much, as long as you can cast it a long way. If you're careful not to spook the school, you can fill your limit within minutes. Some anglers rig their jigs in tandem; this way, they can catch two bass at a time. The surface action lasts well into the fall, sometimes into November.

White bass generally bite best early or late in the day, although a school may start feeding anytime. Surface action is better with overcast skies.

A medium-power spinning outfit, about 6 feet long, with 6-pound-test monofilament is adequate for most white bass fishing, although many anglers use ultralight spinning gear with 4-pound-test line for extra sport.

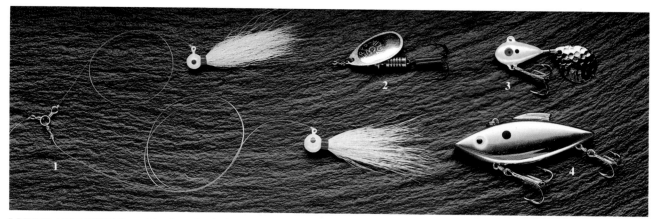

LURES AND RIGS for white bass include: (1) tandem rig, tied on a three-way swivel with 6- and 18-inch leaders of 12-pound mono and ⅛- to ¼-ounce bucktail jigs. The heavy leaders are needed to prevent break-offs should you hook two fish; (2) Mepps Aglia spinner; (3) Little George; (4) Rat-L-Trap.

How to Catch Surface-Feeding White Bass

LURE SIZE is critical. Always use a lure about the size of the baitfish the bass are eating.

APPROACH feeding bass from the upwind side after using binoculars to spot a flock of circling gulls.

STOP well short of the school and begin casting. Often, you'll catch a bass on every cast.

Catfish

Everyone has heard tales of monster catfish that lurk in the muddy waters of the Mississippi. A century ago, many of those stories were probably true, but today, the giant cats are gone — most having fallen victim to the intensive trotline fishery.

Channel cats in the Mississippi run 1½ to 3 pounds; anything over 10 is unusual. Flatheads run larger, with most in the 5- to 15-pound range, and a few up to 30. The Minnesota record channel cat, 38 pounds, was caught in the Mississippi, but in a zone where trotlining is prohibited.

Catfish lie dormant over winter, forming dense schools in certain deep holes in the main channel. They lie flat on the bottom and do not feed. A seine haul in one of these wintering areas produced 2,732 catfish per acre. The cats return to the same holes each winter. Anglers can legally snag the fish in Lake Pepin, but snagging is illegal above and below the lake.

As the water warms and starts to rise in spring, catfish move into the backwaters. Channel cats usually start to bite in late April; flatheads in early May. Look for the fish in holes at least 8 feet deep next to a shallow flat. They often gather around logs or brush. Channel cats feed on shad that have died over the winter, so cut bait, such as sucker cubes or fillets, is very effective. Flatheads prefer whole fish, either alive or fresh, including shad, suckers and bullheads. Anchor and cast into the hole, or if the bottom is not too snaggy, drift through it.

Fish the bait on a slip-sinker rig using a ½- to 1-ounce egg sinker. For channel cats, attach a size 1 or 2 single hook; for flatheads, a 3/0 to 8/0 single hook. Don't be afraid to use big bait. Trotline fishermen have landed big flatheads that had eaten channel cats caught on the line earlier.

By mid-May, the cats are moving shallower. You can catch them at depths of 6 feet or less using slip-sinker rigs baited with whole or cut crayfish for channels and live or fresh fish for flatheads.

Catfish spawn later than most other fish in the river, usually in mid-June, when the water temperature rises into the 70s. They spawn in backwaters and side channels, normally under a ledge, in a hole in the bank or in some place that offers overhead protection. Fishing slows somewhat until spawning is completed and they abandon the heavy cover.

After spawning, most cats move into deep holes in the main channel or side channels, or into holes below the dams. The best spots have plenty of submerged logs and brush for cover.

For channel cats in summer, use a slip-sinker rig with cheesebait, stinkbait, bloodbait, nightcrawlers or leeches. For flatheads, use fresh shad or suckers, either alive or dead. Anchor upstream of holes and snags and fish down into them; tie up to a logjam and dangle the bait vertically between the branches; or fish from the bank.

One of the best summertime patterns for flatheads is to anchor below a dam anytime from late July through August and fish below a closed gate, where the water is flowing back toward the dam. Attach a fresh shad or sucker to a Wolf River rig with a 1- to 4-ounce pyramid sinker. The heavy weight is needed to cast into the restricted area below the gates, and its flat sides and sharp corners help to hold the bait in the current.

In late September, catfish start moving to the deep holes where they will spend the winter. You can catch channel cats on cut shad or suckers; flatheads still prefer whole shad or suckers, the fresher the better. They stop feeding once the water temperature drops below 50° F, usually in mid-October.

As a rule, catfish bite best from sunset to midnight. You may be able to catch some channel cats during the day, but flatheads feed almost exclusively at night. Experienced catfish anglers prefer hot, sticky weather with little rain.

You can catch channel cats on medium-power spinning or baitcasting gear with 8- to 12-pound mono. But flatheads require sturdier tackle, not just because they're larger, but because they spend most of their time in log piles or other snag-infested areas. When you set the hook, you have to turn the fish at once and pull it away from the snag. So most anglers use heavy baitcasting gear with 20- to 35-pound mono or Dacron line.

SUBMERGED LOGS in deep holes along outside bends make ideal habitat for catfish, particularly flatheads.

Cats rest in deep water around the logs during the day, then move shallower at night to feed.

RIGS include: (1) slip-sinker rig, tied with a 1-ounce egg sinker and a size 1 hook baited with stink bait; (2) Wolf

River rig, tied with a three-way swivel, 3-ounce pyramid sinker, and a 5/0 hook baited with a sucker.

Tidewater Rivers

*Because of their link to the sea, tidewater rivers produce gamefish
in tremendous abundance and variety*

At first glance, tidewater rivers resemble other types of warmwater rivers, but the likeness is superficial. The tidal influence causes major differences, not only in the species of fish you can expect to catch, but in when, where and how you fish.

Tidewater rivers usually produce more and bigger fish than similar inland rivers. Most have vast acreages of food-producing flats off the main channel. The marine organisms that inhabit the river also mean a greater variety of food for fish.

To fish these rivers effectively, it helps to understand some basic principles about tides. Tidal fluctuations result mainly from the moon's gravitational pull on the earth's surface (see diagram at right).

This pull creates a bulge of water that stays under the moon as the earth revolves. Centrifugal forces create another bulge of about equal magnitude on the side of the earth opposite the moon. The earth makes one revolution relative to the moon about every 25 hours, and during this time, a given point on the earth experiences a high tide as it passes under the moon, a low tide as it turns away from the moon, another high tide as it passes under the bulge opposite the moon, and another low tide as it turns toward the moon again.

Atlantic coastal waters experience this typical pattern of two highs and lows every 25 hours; a low tide occurs about 6¼ hours after a high. But the angle of the moon, the shape of the ocean's basin and

Cooper River, South Carolina

other geophysical factors may result in a different pattern. Some regions, such as the Gulf coast, experience only one high and one low every 25 hours; the low comes about 12½ hours after the high.

Tides vary considerably in different locations. Some places on earth have tides of 30 feet or more; in others, the tide is only 1 foot. And the amount of

tidal fluctuation changes throughout the month. The greatest fluctuation, called a spring tide, takes place during the full moon and new moon; the smallest (neap tide) occurs during the first and last quarter moon.

Weather conditions along the coast also affect water levels in the river. The levels are higher than nor-

How the Zones of Tidal Influence Change Throughout the Day

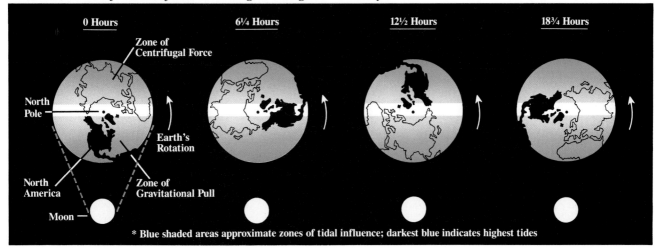

mal with onshore winds; lower with offshore winds. Water levels are higher than normal with a low barometer; lower with a high barometer.

As the tide rises in coastal areas, salt water flows up coastal rivers. The higher the tide, the farther its effects extend upstream. Tidal peaks occur at different times at different points on the river. How fast the tide moves upstream depends on the configuration of the channel; the straighter and deeper it is, the faster the tide progresses.

The downstream reaches of tidewater rivers are nearly as salty as seawater, the middle reaches are brackish, and the upper reaches are fresh. The extent of tidal influence varies in different rivers, depending on the amount of streamflow, gradient of the river channel, and location of dams or waterfalls.

In a high-gradient river, only the lower portion is affected by tides. In a low-gradient river, tidal influence may extend more than 100 miles upstream. Of course, a dam or waterfall prevents tidal influence above that point, assuming the dam or falls is higher than the tidal rise.

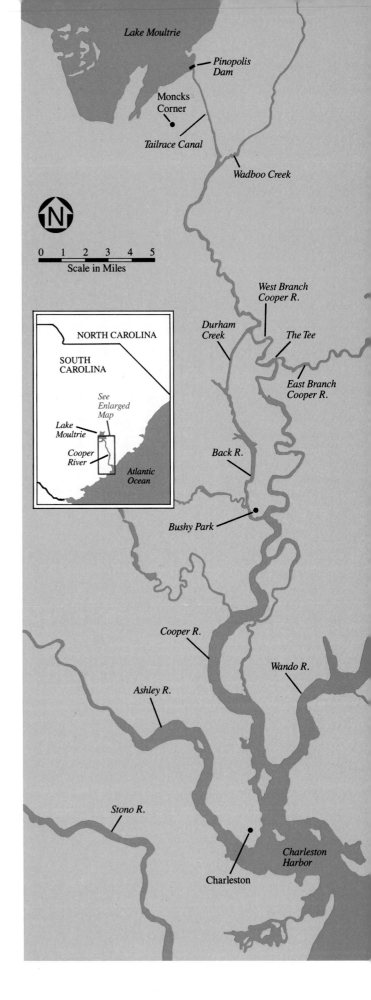

Tide Table: South Carolina Coast

Date		AM	Feet	PM	Feet
Wednesday	Hi	7:43	5.0	8:09	5.7
April 19	Lo	1:39	0.3	1:47	0.3
Thursday	Hi	8:19	5.0	8:45	5.8
April 20	Lo	2:19	0.2	2:23	0.2
Friday	Hi	8:53	4.9	9:19	5.8
April 21	Lo	2:59	0.2	2:57	0.3
Saturday	Hi	9:28	4.7	9:52	5.8
April 22	Lo	3:37	0.3	3:32	0.3
Sunday	Hi	9:59	4.6	10:27	5.7
April 23	Lo	4:16	0.4	4:06	0.4
Monday	Hi	10:33	4.5	11:05	5.7
April 24	Lo	4:55	0.5	4:41	0.5
Tuesday	Hi	11:13	4.5	11:50	5.6
April 25	Lo	5:37	0.7	5:23	0.6

To find times of high and low water add or subtract as indicated.

Sullivan's Island: High, −8 minutes. Low, −12 minutes. Isle of Palms: High, −25 minutes. Low, −28 minutes. Folly Beach: High, −8 minutes. Low, −14 minutes.

Georgetown: High, +1 hour and 34 minutes. Low, +2 hours and 29 minutes. Cape Romain: High, −22 minutes. Low, −17 minutes. McClellanville: High, +27 minutes. Low, +25 minutes. Sewee Bay: High, +13 minutes. Low, +11 minutes. Rockville: High, +19 minutes. Low, +7 minutes.

Beaufort: High, +1 hour and 7 minutes (approximate). Low, +52 minutes (approximate). Edisto Beach: High, −26 minutes (approximate). Low, −35 minutes (approximate).

TIDE TABLES list times of high and low tides and expected tide levels at specific coastal cities or harbors. Tables may also tell you how much time to add for up-river locations or subtract for downriver locations.

Case Study:

Cooper River, South Carolina

INCOMING TIDE means water is flowing into the rice fields. The rising water covers vegetation and old dock posts, and makes it possible to navigate almost anywhere in the field.

The Cooper River in South Carolina's coastal plain is considered one of the top fishing rivers on the Eastern Seaboard. Besides a healthy population of good-sized largemouth bass, the river also supports a tremendous catfish population and plenty of panfish, particularly redears, or shellcrackers. Anglers often catch saltwater species such as redfish, summer flounder, spotted seatrout and striped bass, and there are seasonal runs of American shad and blueback herring.

During the 1700s, giant rice plantations bordered many of the low-country rivers, including the Cooper. Dikes separated the rice paddies from the main channel, and water levels in the paddies were regulated by wooden gates on channels leading to the river. The plantations relied on slave labor to maintain the paddies and harvest the rice.

The Civil War ended the plantation system, and the paddies started to deteriorate. Eventually, the dikes and control gates washed out, leaving a vast network of backwater lakes whose water level changed in concert with the river. Today these backwaters, which are still called "rice fields," attract many species of gamefish.

The cuts, or breaks, leading into the rice fields make excellent feeding areas, as do the ditches across the fields. Dug to allow passage of rice boats, the ditches make ideal havens for bass, especially at low tide. And the extra depth makes it easier to run a motor.

The Cooper River arises from two branches. The West Branch gets most of its flow from Lake Moultrie (one of the Santee-Cooper lakes). The Lake Moultrie discharge flows through a man-made tailrace canal for 4 miles before joining Wadboo Creek to form the West Branch. The West Branch then flows on for 12 miles before joining the East Branch. The junction of the two branches is called the "Tee." The main branch then flows to the south for 33 miles, joining the Ashley and Wando rivers near the lower end before emptying into Charleston Harbor.

The Pinopolis Dam, which forms Lake Moultrie, is a hydroelectric dam. When water is released to gen-

OUTGOING TIDE means water is flowing out of the rice fields. As the water level drops, vegetation and dock posts become exposed, and boat fishermen oblivious to the tides are trapped in water too shallow to navigate.

Cooper River Physical Data (downstream of the Tee)

Average width	700 ft
Average depth	20 ft
Gradient	low
Clarity	2 ft
Color	brown
Discharge (cubic feet per second)	4,500
Winter low temperature	43° F
Summer high temperature	88° F

erate electricity, the river rises. Both high and low tides are higher when electricity is being generated.

In 1985, the U.S. Army Corps of Engineers completed a canal to divert 70 percent of the Cooper River's flow into the nearby Santee River. The idea was to reduce the rate at which the Cooper deposited silt into Charleston Harbor. The Corps, however, miscalculated the effects of the diversion. The result was greater saltwater intrusion than originally intended. Besides rusting out the equipment of many factories along the river, the salt water changed the mix of fish species. Each year saltwater species move farther and farther upriver. Recently, anglers reported a school of jack crevalle in the tailrace of the Pinopolis Dam.

Although saltwater fish are becoming more common in the upper river, most are still found in the lower 20 miles. Largemouth bass, white perch, channel catfish and occasionally blue catfish are caught below the Tee. But it is unusual to find other freshwater species that far downstream because they are not as salt tolerant.

FRESHWATER SPECIES	SALT TOLERANCE
Largemouth bass	high
Channel catfish	high
White perch	high
Blue catfish	moderate
Redear sunfish	moderate
Flathead catfish	low
Bluegill	low
Redbreast sunfish	low
Black crappie	low

SALTWATER SPECIES	FRESHWATER TOLERANCE
Summer flounder	high
Striped bass	high
Red drum	moderate
Spotted seatrout	moderate

Cooper River Habitat

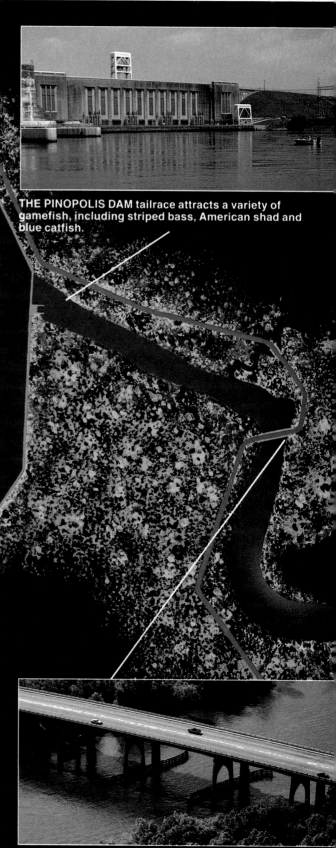

THE PINOPOLIS DAM tailrace attracts a variety of gamefish, including striped bass, American shad and blue catfish.

BRIDGES, especially those with wood pilings alongside the concrete piers, break the current and provide good cover for gamefish.

RICE FIELDS are ideal spots for large-mouth bass and panfish to avoid the current and find cover.

DITCHES in rice fields offer bass and panfish a deepwater refuge when the tide is low.

CUTS into the rice fields are feeding spots for a variety of fish. Many have wooden pilings for cover.

DEEP HOLES, along outside bends or near rice field cuts, hold catfish, stripers and, in winter, largemouths.

VEGETATION along the river's edge makes excellent panfish cover, especially around spawning time.

FEEDER CREEKS and canals draw largemouth bass and panfish, often to the upper ends, at spawning time.

Cooper River:

Sunfish

Northern anglers would be astounded to see a typical stringer of Cooper River shellcrackers. At spawning time, it's not unusual to catch dozens of 1½- to 2-pounders from a single spawning bed. Besides shellcrackers (redear sunfish), the river holds good numbers of bluegill and redbreast sunfish.

Shellcrackers spawn around the full moon in April and again in May. Fishing peaks a day or two either side of the full moon. Fishing is also good around the new moon. Bluegills spawn from late May to late June; redbreasts, from early May to early June. Bluegills and redbreasts, too, spawn around the full moon.

You'll find shellcrackers spawning along the edge of the river, most often where bulrushes grow with the usual stands of arrowhead, cutgrass, maidencane and pickerelweed. The rushes require a firm bottom, just as the fish do for spawning. Shellcrackers also spawn in this type of vegetation in some tributary creeks and canals.

Bluegills and redbreasts spawn in rice field ditches, usually in areas out of the current.

Experienced anglers claim they can sniff out sunfish spawning beds. Biologists explain that the smell comes from the milt of spawning males. Wiggling

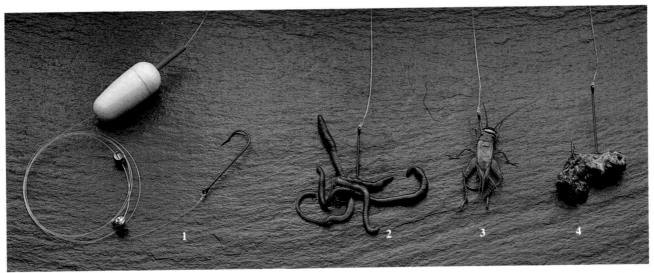

RIGS AND BAITS include: (1) bobber rig with a size 4 Aberdeen hook. For shellcrackers, bait up with (2) three red wigglers hooked through the middle. For bluegills and redbreasts, with a (3) cricket hooked through the body and out the rear of the abdomen, or a (4) catalpa worm turned inside out.

How to Fish Shellcrackers at Spawning Time

1. SNIFF OUT the spawning beds by motoring along slowly, always moving into the wind. The smell resembles that of a fish market.

2. ANCHOR when you find a spawning bed. Drop an anchor at each end to keep the boat parallel to the edge of the weeds, within easy reach of an extension pole.

3. DABBLE a bobber rig and worms into pockets in the weeds. Work one pocket for a minute or two, then try another. If the fish are around, they'll bite right away.

4. LIFT the fish straight up after setting the hook. If you let it run too far, it may tangle the line around tough-stemmed weeds.

LOOK for redbreasts (above) and bluegills around woody cover. Submerged logs, fallen trees, brush and old dock pilings provide shade, shelter from the current, and protection from predatory fish.

bulrushes are another sign of fish. If you can't smell the fish or see the rushes move, you can locate a bed by drifting slowly along the edge of the river. Dabble your bait into pockets in the weeds with a 12-foot cane pole or fiberglass extension pole.

Tie to the tip a length of 14-pound line as long as the pole. Then thread on a small float, pinch on a split-shot or two, and add a size 4 Aberdeen hook. For shellcrackers, bait up with two or three red wigglers; use crickets for bluegills and redbreasts.

The best time to catch sunfish is around low tide. Falling water forces the fish to the edge of the weeds, where you can easily place your bait. As the tide rises, the fish move back into the weeds, where you'll have trouble reaching them. If you snag up, the 14-pound line will enable you to pull free. And you can pull out a big sunfish before it burrows into the vegetation.

After spawning, sunfish move deeper. You'll find them in the main channel at depths of 6 to 15 feet, usually at the edge of the weeds or in woody cover.

Shellcrackers and redbreasts hug bottom; bluegills may be suspended. Often, sunfish congregate around the mouth of a rice field cut.

The easiest way to locate sunfish after the spawning period and through the summer is to troll slowly along the edge of the weeds with an electric motor. Use a 6½- to 7-foot spinning outfit with 8-pound mono. Rig up as you would at spawning time, omitting the float and adding enough split-shot to keep your line vertical. Fish just off the edge of the weeds, but drop your bait into any pockets along the weed margin. Keep moving until you find the fish.

Some of the biggest sunfish are caught on summer nights using a technique called "glow poppin'." Work the edges of the weeds in quiet water using a small glow-in-the-dark popper.

In fall and winter, you'll find sunfish near the same spots as in summer, but slightly deeper. Troll along the edge of the channel using the same live-bait rigs. On a warm day, the fish move back into the weeds.

Tips for Finding and Catching Sunfish

CATCH big sunfish at night by flipping a glow-in-the-dark popper into pockets along the weed edges using an extension pole. Move along slowly with an electric motor or scull with oars to avoid spooking the fish.

ATTACH a size 2 clip-on spinner to your hook for extra attraction. The spinner provides enough weight that you can eliminate the split-shot.

WORK the area around culverts for bluegills and red-breasts. Sunfish are attracted by the inflowing water and the food it washes in.

Cooper River:
Largemouth Bass

Everyone in the Southeast has heard about the great bass fishing in the Santee-Cooper lakes, but few know how good Cooper River bass fishing can be.

Most local anglers concentrate on the lakes, where the fishing is not complicated by the influence of the tides. Those who have taken time to learn the river, however, have equally good success. And they can fish the river on many days when high winds keep anglers off the big water.

Like all fish in the Cooper River system, bass grow big. Seven- to nine-pounders are not unusual, and the river has produced fish over 12 pounds. Medium to heavy baitcasting tackle with 14- to 20-pound line is recommended for extracting big bass from the heavy weeds and woody cover common on the river.

You can catch Cooper River bass year around. Most of them winter in deep holes adjacent to the rice fields, but starting in early March, they move into the cuts leading into the fields.

The best rice fields are those with current running in one end and out the other. Depth is also important. If the field becomes nearly dry at low tide, chances are it won't hold many bass at high tide. The cuts, however, may still hold some fish.

On an incoming tide, stay on the inside of the cuts and cast out toward the channel using a crawfish-pattern crankbait. On an outgoing tide, stay on the outside and cast into the cuts. Another good bait for working the cuts is a chartreuse spinnerbait.

As the water warms, bass move farther back in the rice fields, although some can still be found around the cuts. By late March or early April, when the water temperature reaches 65° F, bass begin bedding in ditches in the rice fields or on weedy rice field flats. They also spawn in tributary creeks and man-made canals. Spawning activity peaks in mid- to late April. Bass stay in the vicinity of bedding areas for several weeks after spawning is completed.

One popular springtime technique is casting buzz-baits around bedding areas. Starting about three hours before low tide, work buzzbaits over weed patches on the flats. Then, as low tide approaches, move to the ditches. Good fishing usually continues for about 1½ hours into the rising tide. You can also catch bass in spring on Texas-rigged floating worms, using only a barrel swivel for weight; floating minnow plugs fished on the surface with a twitch-and-wait retrieve; or spinnerbaits, although they tend to foul in the thick weed patches. Another

How to Work the Cuts

CURRENT

POSITION your boat on the river side of the cut and cast from the outside in on the outgoing tide. This way, your lure moves with the current, just like natural food

drifting out of the rice fields. On the incoming tide, position your boat on the rice field side, cast out toward the river and work the lure in.

good technique, especially at high tide, is casting over the weedtops with noise-producing vibrating plugs, such as Rat-L-Traps or Rattl'n Raps.

Experts advocate fishing in moving water throughout the year. When the tide goes slack, run up- or down-river to find a spot where the water is flowing.

Fishing can be tough in summer, and the bass usually run smaller. By late May, water temperatures rise into the upper 70s and bass feed more often at night. As the summer progresses and water temperatures approach the 90s, most feeding is at night.

You can catch some bass during the day, however, by fishing the cuts on an outgoing tide. Bass lie along the outside edge of the cut, waiting for food to wash out to them. Cast a Texas-rigged plastic worm into the cut, then drift it slowly along the bottom with the current. Topwater baits, especially floating minnow plugs, may be effective in early morning.

On summer nights, fish the rice fields using noisy surface baits, such as crawlers, chuggers and buzz-baits. Big Texas-rigged worms also work well because they imitate the eels found in the river. Dark colors, especially black, are the best choice. At high tide, work the weedtops; low tide, the ditches.

As the water begins to cool in fall, you'll find bass in rice field ditches, cuts, and outside bends adja-cent to rice fields. The best fall spots have hard, sandy bottoms with water 6 to 8 feet deep.

By early October, bass are feeding heavily on shad, so experts rely on crankbaits and jigging spoons. Work them around points that form the cuts leading into the rice fields. At night, you can catch bass in the same cuts, only in shallower water.

By mid-December, the water drops below 55° F, and bass move into deep holes in the main channel adjacent to cuts in the rice fields. The holes vary in depth from 10 to 35 feet. You can catch good numbers of bass by hovering over these holes and jigging vertically with a shad-imitating jig, jig-and-pig, vibrating blade or jigging spoon. On an outgoing tide, you can catch some bass by casting into the cuts with a jig or jigging spoon and letting the current wash it out.

Winter fishing is best when water is being discharged from the Pinopolis Dam. The current draws bass to the holes, where they can easily ambush food that drifts by. Without current, the bass scatter in search of food, making them difficult to find.

Many Cooper River anglers consider winter the peak time for largemouth bass, especially for big ones. The deepwater winter fishing lasts until early March, when bass begin moving into shallow water in preparation for spawning.

How to Fish a Buzzbait

LOWER your rod tip as the lure nears the boat. Keeping the tip high would pull the blade out of the water.

BEGIN your retrieve with your rod tip high after casting to weedy cover in the rice fields.

DELAY setting the hook until you feel extra weight. The tendency is to set the hook at any swirl or splash; if you do, you'll probably pull the lure away from the fish.

LURES AND RIGS include: (1) Lehi worm Texas-rigged, (2) Triple Wing buzzbait, (3) Houston Model spinnerbait, (4) Bang-O-Lure, (5) Ivie's Shad, (6) Deep Wee R, (7) Rattl'n Rap, (8) Stanley Jig and pork frog, (9) Strata Spoon.

NIGHT FISHING is the best way to catch bass in summer. Around high tide, fish weed patches in the rice fields. Use noisy surface lures or plastic worms, all in black or dark colors.

Bass-Fishing Tips

WORK your lure across points that form cuts. Here, bass can get out of the current, yet be in position to grab shad, crayfish or other food passing through the cut.

CAST to dock posts or any kind of stick-ups around the cuts or in the rice fields themselves. The posts may be the only woody cover available to bass.

Cooper River:
Catfish

Catfish grow big in the Cooper River — and there are lots of them. Most catfish anglers who fish the river regularly have at least one 50-pounder to their credit. In 1988, the river produced an 86-pound, 4-ounce blue catfish, a South Carolina record.

Besides blues, the Cooper also supports some channel cats and a few flathead and white cats. But blues grow much larger and draw the most attention.

Cooper River cats bite all year, although most fishing is done in spring and summer. During the spawning period, early to mid-May, the cats move shallower, but otherwise you'll find them in the same areas all year. And you can use the same fishing techniques year around.

Most of the fish are found in deep holes, mainly from the Pinopolis Dam downstream to Bushy Park, although some blues are found in the river's extreme lower reaches.

The depth of the best holes varies from 15 to 65 feet; the holes should be at least 5 feet deeper than the surrounding water. Generally, the holes are located just downstream of a break leading into a rice field, or along outside bends of the main channel.

You'll need powerful tackle to handle these big cats. Most anglers prefer a heavy spinning or bait-casting outfit with 40- to 50-pound mono. Use a three-way swivel rig or a slip-sinker rig; a three-way rig keeps your bait farther off bottom, where cats can see it better. And should you get snagged, the lighter dropper allows you to break off the sinker without losing the rest of the rig.

Any kind of baitfish native to the river, including golden shiners, bream, menhaden and mullet, will catch cats, but most experts prefer herring when they are available. Whatever the bait, it should be fresh. Herring and mullet are usually cut into chunks, but may be fished live. For smaller cats, use shelled shrimp tails or catalpa worms.

Position your boat at the upstream edge of a hole, lower the bait to the bottom, then let your boat drift slowly through the hole. Use a trolling motor to control your drift. On a windy day, anchor your boat upstream and cast into the hole. If the cats don't bite in 10 to 15 minutes, try another hole.

The best time to catch cats is around high or low tide. During these periods, the tide is fairly slack, so you can control your bait more easily. The water is clearer, too, so the fish can see your bait better. Cats will bite almost anytime, day or night, but fishing is usually best during stable weather.

How to Rig up for Catfish

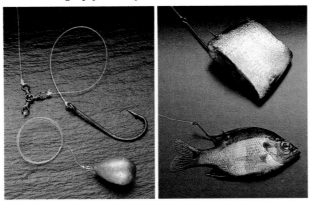

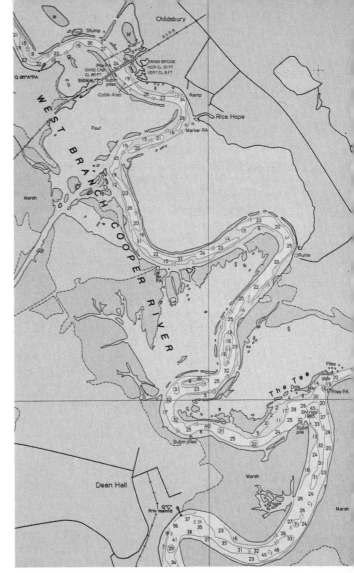

TIE a three-way swivel rig using 50-pound mono; an 8-inch, 50-pound leader with an 8/0 hook; and a 2-foot, 20-pound dropper with a 3-ounce sinker. Hook cut bait (above right) as shown; whole sunfish (below right) and herring through the back; menhaden and shad through the lips.

NAUTICAL CHARTS showing bottom contours can help you locate good catfish holes. The maps also show features such as navigation aids and bottom types. Maps like the one above are available from the National Ocean Service in Riverdale, Maryland.

Catfishing Tips

SLOW your drift by lowering a sash weight off the bow of your boat. The weight also keeps the boat drifting lengthwise, parallel to shore.

ATTACH a jug to your anchor rope when fishing for big cats. This way, when a big one hits, you can untie the rope, toss it into the water (left), and follow the fish (right). After landing the cat, motor back to your jug and anchor up in the exact position where you caught the fish.

Cooper River:
Striped Bass

As in most coastal rivers, striped bass runs in the Cooper have declined in recent years. But you can still catch them if you know where to look. Cooper River stripers run 7 to 8 pounds, but there's a chance of catching fish up to 45 pounds.

In late February, stripers begin moving into the tailrace of the Pinopolis Dam, where they will spawn. To protect the spawners, a closed area has been established from the dam to 175 yards downstream. Anglers using jigs catch a few stripers just downstream

LURES for Cooper River striped bass include: (1) Bomber Long A, (2) Bagley Bang-O-B, (3) Mann's 30+, (4) ¾-ounce banana-head bucktail jig tipped with an Ivie's Shad, and (5) Bett's Bucktail Worm.

from the closed area, but fishing is slow because of the reduced numbers of fish.

After spawning, stripers begin working their way downstream. Some, however, stay in the closed area all year. Once the fish leave the dam, they are difficult to find. By October, most have moved downstream to the brackish water. Seldom will you catch one above the Tee.

Fishing peaks in December and January, with the best catches coming at night. The exact tide is not too important, although slack tides are not good. There should be enough current to flush food out of the deep holes.

Look for striped bass in deep eddies that form along outside bends, around docks or bridge piers, and below rock piles. Stripers in deep eddies do not have to fight the current, yet they can easily ambush baitfish hanging along the current margin. Other good spots include shelves downstream from deep holes, and lighted piers adjacent to deep water. All are prime feeding areas.

Two techniques account for most stripers: casting with jigs and trolling with plugs. Jigs are best for working specific objects, such as piers, or where the water is too deep for trolling. With either technique, use a 6- to 7-foot heavy baitcasting outfit with 20- to 25-pound mono.

For jigging, tie on a ½- to ¾-ounce jig, hold the boat just below the spot you want to fish, cast upstream, then bounce the jig slowly with the current. When running the river, be on the lookout for jumping menhaden or shrimp. If you see surface activity, it could mean feeding stripers. Stop and make a few casts with a jig.

Trolling works better than casting when the fish are scattered. Troll slowly against the current using big-lipped crankbaits that will reach bottom at depths of 20 to 30 feet. If you troll with the current, you'll snag up more often, and the plugs won't have as much action. You can also use these deep-diving crankbaits for casting to specific spots, such as eddies and rock piles.

Striper Hotspots

BRIDGES, especially those nearest the Pinopolis Dam, are striper magnets. Baitfish concentrate in the eddies and around the wooden pilings, making a natural feeding area for stripers in the tailrace.

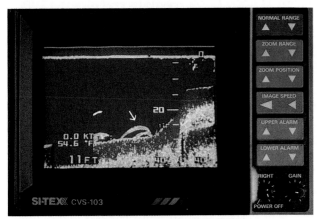

SHELVES downstream from deep holes make ideal feeding areas for stripers. The fish (arrow) rest in the holes during the day and then move up on 10- to 12-foot flats in the evening to feed.

ROCKY AREAS, such as riprap shorelines, submerged rock piles and ruins of old buildings, are good feeding spots for stripers. Baitfish are attracted by the insect larvae that live among the rocks.

Cooper River:
Shad

These sporty fish spend their life at sea, returning to coastal rivers each spring to spawn. Shad migrate to the Cooper River from locations as distant as Nova Scotia.

The main attraction, in terms of numbers and size, is the American shad. Anglers catch plenty of 4- to 5-pounders and someone occasionally lands one over 6. The river also draws a few hickory shad, which are considerably smaller.

In a mild winter, the fish move into the river in late December, concentrating below the Pinopolis Dam. In a severe winter, they may not appear until April. Normally, the run peaks a few days either side of the full moon in March, with the males (buck shad) showing up first and the females (roe shad) about two weeks later.

Look for shad in swift current, usually where it brushes against a point or flows over a bar. You'll seldom find them in slack water.

Anchor just upstream and cast a jig or shad dart weighing 1/16- to 1/4-ounce, depending on the current speed. Let the lure sink to the bottom, then retrieve slowly. Use a more erratic retrieve in slower current. If the fish aren't on the bottom, try counting the jig down to different depths before starting your retrieve. Another good technique is simply casting a light jig downstream and allowing it to flutter in the current.

Most shad anglers prefer light spinning gear with 4- to 6-pound mono. Make sure your drag is set properly, because shad are powerful fighters, sometimes making 8 or 10 spectacular leaps before giving in. They have paper-thin flesh around their mouths, so the hook will tear out easily if you try to horse them in. Land them with a long-handled dip net.

Shad fishing is best when the current is strongest, usually midway between high and low tides. Fishing generally picks up when water is being discharged from the Pinopolis Dam.

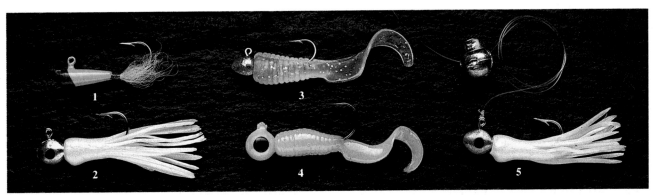

LURES AND RIGS include: (1) Shad Dart, (2) Original Mini Jig, (3) Mann's Curly-Tail Grub, and (4) Mister Twister Teeny, all in 1/16- to 1/8-ounce sizes. When fishing in swift water, (5) pinch on a 1/4-ounce split-shot about a foot above your jig. This way, you can get down to the fish without using a jig too large for them.

Where to Find Cooper River Shad

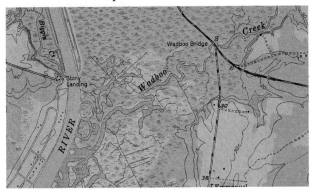

WADBOO CREEK was a shad spawning area before the tailrace canal was built, and it still draws some shad.

PINOPOLIS DAM tailrace is the major shad-fishing area. The dam blocks the shad's upstream migration.

POWER PLANT discharge canal north of Bushy Park attracts shad because the water is constantly moving.

Cooper River:
Other Species

Besides the fish species already mentioned, the Cooper River offers a smorgasbord of other freshwater and saltwater fishes. It's possible to catch black crappies, spotted sunfish (stumpknockers), white perch (not to be confused with the local name for white crappie), red drum (spottail or channel bass), spotted seatrout, summer flounder and blueback herring. There are occasional reports of jack crevalle, winter flounder and even small tarpon.

Although saltwater fish are scarce above Bushy Park, there has been a definite upriver shift in populations of many saltwater species, particularly red drum, since the diversion canal was built.

Freshwater Species

WHITE PERCH run big in the Cooper, from ¾ to 2½ pounds. They're found throughout the entire river. Anglers catch them in and around cuts and creek mouths on two-hook bottom rigs baited with cut shrimp. Fishing is good from May to October.

SPOTTED SUNFISH are common in the Cooper, running from ¼ to ½ pound. Excellent eating, they can be caught from May to September around stumps and cypress trees in stagnant backwaters as far downriver as the power plant. Crickets make good bait.

BLACK CRAPPIES bite best from mid-March to mid-April. They're found as far downstream as the power plant north of Bushy Park. You can catch them by jigging in deep eddies along steep banks. The fish average 1½ pounds and top out at 3½, but numbers have declined greatly in recent years.

SPOTTED SEATROUT are found upstream to Bushy Park, with the heaviest run from October through December. They average 2 pounds, with a few up to 6. They move into creeks on the incoming tide; to creek mouths on the outgoing. Troll with a jig-grub combo.

RED DRUM are most common around Bushy Park. They average 5 pounds. They lie along weed edges and on weedy flats on the incoming tide; around the mouths of cuts on the outgoing. Use shrimp, menhaden or mullet on a jig or split-shot rig. Fishing is best from May to October.

SUMMER FLOUNDER migrate upriver as far as the Pinopolis Dam. You'll find them near the bank or up on weedy flats on the incoming tide; away from the bank or around creek mouths on the outgoing. Most summer flounder are caught from May to October on menhaden or shrimp on a split-shot rig.

Southern Largemouth Rivers

Dams have impounded many southern rivers, but there's still plenty of free-flowing water teeming with bass

When you mention bass fishing in the South, most folks automatically think of the famous southern reservoirs — sprawling man-made lakes, such as Bull Shoals, Percy Priest and Truman. The idea of river fishing is foreign to most.

But many of the rivers feeding the reservoirs had good numbers of gamefish long before the dams were built, and the free-flowing portions of these rivers still hold plenty of fish. And not just bass, but also catfish, crappies, sunfish and introduced species, such as stripers.

Although the dams have destroyed enormous amounts of habitat for stream-dwelling species, fishing has actually improved in much of the free-flowing water that remains. The reservoirs reduce the intensity of flooding in the rivers, minimizing bank erosion and giving weedbeds a better chance to develop. Tailwaters of the dams are concentration points for a variety of gamefish, especially during spring spawning runs. And the reservoirs produce tremendous quantities of fish, some of which migrate upstream into the free-flowing rivers at certain times of the year.

The average southern angler avoids river fishing because he feels he can catch fish more consistently in the lakes. It's true that river fish are more difficult to locate and catch because of constantly changing conditions, but anglers skilled at fishing moving water know there are times when a river is the better choice.

In windy weather, for instance, a good-sized reservoir is tough to fish and may even be treacherous; rivers are fishable even in a high wind. To get out of the wind, simply move around a bend. Also, river fish seem less affected by cold fronts and thunderstorms, conditions that usually cause lake fishing to shut down.

Pearl River, Mississippi

Case Study:
Pearl River, Mississippi

The Pearl River, which splits the southern half of Mississippi before emptying into the Gulf of Mexico, is typical of many southern rivers. Approximately 150 miles below the headwaters, the Ross Barnett Dam backs up water for 36 miles, forming a 33,000-acre reservoir of the same name. Below the dam, the lower river flows on for more than 300 miles, spilling into the Gulf near Port Bienville.

Although the upper and lower river both offer excellent fishing, the emphasis in this book will be on the upper river because it typifies hundreds of small to medium-sized rivers found throughout the South. Also included will be information on fishing the tailrace, below the reservoir.

The upper river, from the town of Philadelphia to the Ross Barnett Reservoir, meanders slowly through mixed hardwood and conifer forest as well as tupelo gum and cypress swamps. The channel, which averages about 120 feet wide and 12 feet deep, is laced with deadfalls, submerged stumps and towering cypress trees. The bottom consists mainly of sand, clay and silt, and the water carries a heavy silt load

at all times, even when the river is low. At normal stage, the visibility may be 2 to 3 feet; at high water, only 6 inches. By comparison, the lower river is wider, deeper and somewhat clearer. It meanders much more, and the lower 13 miles are influenced by the tides.

Along the upper river's course are numerous sloughs connected to the main channel by narrow cuts. The sloughs are actually the lower ends of tributary streams, although some are oxbow lakes that have not completely separated from the river.

Most of the upper river is navigable in a fishing boat, although some stretches require a very small boat or a canoe. About 24 miles above the reservoir, a low-head dam restricts boat traffic. The 4-foot-high dam is intended to raise the water level upstream for better navigability.

Important fish in this stretch include largemouth and spotted (Kentucky) bass, white crappies (white perch), black crappies, bluegills (bream), channel catfish, blue catfish, flathead catfish (tabby cats), wipers (striped bass–white bass hybrids), and occasionally striped bass.

**Pearl River Physical Data
(at low-head dam)**

Average width	120 ft
Average depth	12 ft
Gradient	low
Clarity	2 to 3 ft
Color	brown
Discharge (cubic feet per second)	450
Winter low temperature	45° F
Summer high temperature	90° F

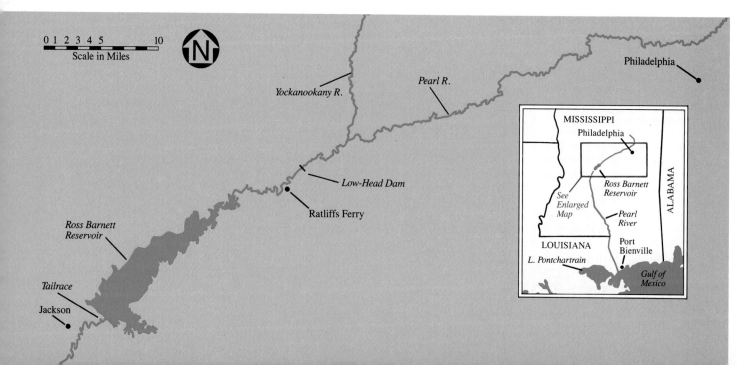

SANDY POINTS in the main channel make good feeding areas for spotted bass and catfish.

POINTS at a slough junction attract bass and crappies, especially if there are weeds and stumps.

OXBOW SLOUGHS remain when the river changes course. They make ideal habitat for bass and panfish.

CREEK MOUTH SLOUGHS connected to the river make ideal spawning areas for largemouth bass and crappies.

DEEP CUTS connecting sloughs to the river appeal to crappies, largemouth bass and spotted bass.

LOW-HEAD DAM blocks upstream migration, so it concentrates migratory fish, such as wipers.

Pearl River:
Largemouth Bass

Anglers accustomed to catching largemouth bass in clear lakes or reservoirs may have a hard time adjusting to the murky waters of the upper Pearl. Because of the low visibility, the fish spend their entire life in shallow water, seldom venturing below 8 feet.

But it's well worth learning how to catch them since the river receives much less fishing pressure than the reservoir. The bass are good-sized, but not huge, averaging about 2 pounds with an occasional fish up to 7.

Although some local anglers consider the upper portion of the reservoir to be part of the river, the information that follows pertains only to the free-flowing portion upstream from Ratliffs Ferry.

Starting in late March, largemouths move into the sloughs where the warm, slack water and thick beds of lily pads offer good conditions for spawning. Normally, they spawn in water less than a foot deep. The cuts leading into the sloughs also hold bass this time of year; deeper cuts with good cover hold bass all year.

The best lures for this shallow cover include buzzbaits and weedless frogs, but spinnerbaits, plastic lizards and minnow plugs twitched on the surface also produce plenty of bass. When the fish go deeper, try a jig-and-pig. Most local anglers prefer flippin' sticks with 17- to 30-pound mono, but a 5½-foot medium-power baitcasting outfit with 14- to 17-pound mono is better for working minnow plugs.

In early May, bass start moving out to the main river to feed on shad. Look for them around lily pad points at slough mouths, eddies at the edge of the main channel, undercut banks, log and brush piles, and standing cypress trees. To attract fish, any of these spots must adjoin deep water.

Early or late in the day or in overcast weather, you can catch bass on the same shallow-water lures as in spring, but crankbaits or plastic worms work better on sunny days when the bass go deeper.

You'll find bass in these locations through the fall and winter, although they move a little deeper when the water dips into the mid-50s. The fish may move back into the sloughs after a heavy rain if the current in the river becomes too swift. When the water is falling, look for bass where the cuts empty into the main river.

As the water cools in fall, bass will roam farther from cover. Work a larger area around obstructions and retrieve more slowly than you would in summer. Once the water temperature drops into the low 60s, surface lures are no longer effective. A jig-and-pig is the best overall choice, although crankbaits work well in light cover.

The peak times for largemouths on the Pearl are from May through early July, and October through December. Early spring fishing may be tough, because the water is often high and muddy. Fishing is best when the river is within its banks and falling slowly.

1. CAST a weedless frog into openings in the lily pads; wait for the ripples to subside.

2. SKIP the frog across the lily pads, letting it lie for several seconds in each opening.

3. PAUSE when you see a boil, then set the hook. If you set too soon, the fish may not have the lure.

4. PULL the largemouth's head upward to prevent the fish from diving into the lily pad stems.

LURES AND RIGS include: (1) Spoiler Lizard, Texas-rigged, with ⅛-ounce bullet sinker; (2) Toledo Worm, Texas-rigged, with ⅛-ounce bullet sinker; (3) Toledo Worm, Carolina-rigged, with a ¾-ounce bullet sinker; (4) Snagproof Frog; (5) Racket Buzz; (6) Bang-O-Lure; (7) Stanley Jig tipped with a pork frog; (8) Bitty B.

Tips for Catching Largemouths

LOOK for stumps among the weeds in sloughs or on points at creek junctions. The stumps provide better cover for bass than the weeds alone.

USE a buzzbait with styrofoam floats (inset) so you can slow your retrieve without the lure sinking.

SPRAY a soft-plastic lizard with oil-based scent to make it slide through the weeds without fouling.

Pearl River:
Spotted Bass

When fishing the upper Pearl, you may hook a fish that looks much like a largemouth, but fights with the stamina of a smallmouth. Called "spots" by local anglers, these never-give-up battlers are actually spotted bass. They're also known as "Kentuckies."

Spots are often found in the same places as largemouths, but they will tolerate more current. They don't average quite as big, although the river has produced spots over 6 pounds.

In mid- to late March, when the water temperature hits the mid-60s, spots move into cuts leading into the sloughs or into eddies along the main channel. Most of the fish spawn in pockets in brushy cover, usually at inner ends of the cuts, or in the sloughs.

As a rule, lures for spots should be smaller than those for largemouths. The most effective lures in springtime cover, such as brush or lily pads, are ⅛-ounce spinnerbaits and 4-inch lizards. In lighter cover, you can catch spots on small crankbaits and vibrating plugs.

Some spots hang around the cuts all summer. Others move onto sandy points above outside bends or into deep pools in the bends. Although the fish may go as deep as 20 feet in summer, most are caught at depths of 6 to 8 feet.

Medium-diving crankbaits and plastic worms provide most of the summertime action. In deep pools or cuts with few snags, or on clean sandbars, use a Carolina rig; in brushy cover, a Texas rig.

Beginning in October, shad congregate below the low-head dam and spots are close behind. You'll find them in the turbulent water directly below the dam, or around points, cuts and outside bends in the first mile downstream of the dam. The fish remain in these locations into December. Use crankbaits when fishing below the dam; otherwise, use the same lures as in summer.

Winter is the best time for big spots. Work sharp breaks along outside bends, particularly where there is woody cover on a 6- to 8-foot-deep shelf. One favorite wintertime lure is the Whing Ding, a type of tailspin with a body that can slide up the line, making it more difficult for a bass to throw the hook. Cast it to the bank and retrieve with 3-foot lifts, letting it hit bottom each time. Spots strike as the lure is sinking, so keep your line taut on the drop. This presentation lets you cover a lot of water in a hurry. Once you find the fish, try a slower presentation with a jig-and-pig or plastic worm.

A good all-around outfit for spots is a medium-heavy baitcasting rod and matching reel spooled with 12- to 14-pound mono. This outfit is heavy enough to horse spots from thick cover yet will still cast fairly light lures.

Spots are easiest to find and catch when the water is low because they're concentrated in eddies, and the water is clear enough to see the bait easily.

LURES AND RIGS for spotted bass include: (1) Bitty B; (2) Whing Ding; (3) Rat-L-Trap; (4) Phenom Worm, rigged Carolina-style, weighted with a ¾-ounce bullet sinker; (5) Mepps Bass Killer; (6) Bagley Kil'r B2; (7) Super Lizard, rigged Texas-style, weighted with a ¼-ounce bullet sinker; (8) Stanley Jig tipped with a pork frog; and (9) Phenom Worm, rigged Texas-style, weighted with a ⅜-ounce bullet sinker.

Prime Locations for Spots

DEEP CUTS connecting the river to the sloughs are good spotted-bass producers. With your boat at the mouth of the cut, cast a medium-diving crankbait to the points on either side, then make a few casts down the middle.

SANDY POINTS that have lots of woody cover and drop sharply into the main channel hold spots from late August into December. Work the wood with spinnerbaits, crankbaits, or plastic worms.

SLAB SPOONS (see below) are ideal for catching hybrids in the tailrace. With a 1-ounce spoon and 12-pound mono, you can cast up to 200 feet to reach the fast water in the middle of the river.

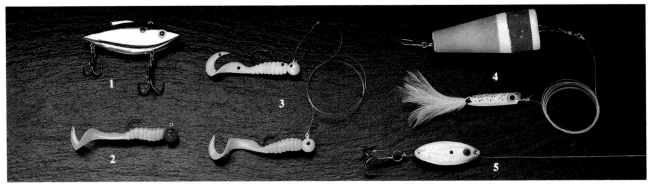

LURES AND RIGS for wipers include: (1) Rat-L-Trap; (2) ¼-ounce twister-tail jig; (3) tandem rig, tied with 12-pound mono and a pair of ¼-ounce jigs, one attached to a loop 12 to 18 inches up the line; (4) Glow Top Popping Float with an 18- to 24-inch leader of 14-pound mono and a Buck's Top Striper jig; and (5) Skipper Shad.

Pearl River:
Wipers

When the wipers are running in the Ross Barnett tailrace, you're likely to see bank fishermen standing elbow to elbow. Often, several are battling fish at the same time. This hectic scene is repeated each spring, normally from late February to late May.

Wipers are actually striped bass–white bass hybrids or, to many folks, simply "hybrids." These gamy fighters, running from 3 to 14 pounds, prefer the fast water immediately below the dam. The smaller ones can be caught in the margins of the eddies on either side of the fast water, but the bigger fish stay in the swift water in the middle of the river.

When the water warms in summer, wipers leave the tailrace and scatter downstream. But they return again in fall, usually in September, and fishing stays good until late December. Many consider fall the best time for big wipers.

To fish the tailrace effectively, you'll need surf-casting tackle or baitcasting gear suitable for making 150- to 200-foot casts, and 10- to 14-pound mono. Some local anglers modify their baitcasting reels by removing the gear grease and substituting WD-40. Many fishermen use a specially designed, lead-bodied slab spoon. The line threads through the body, and when a fish strikes and shakes its head, the lure slides up the line. This way, the fish cannot use the weight of the lure to throw the hook. Not only is the lure easy to cast, it's shaped like a shad, the hybrids' usual prey.

Weighted popping corks, or "agitators," also add casting distance, and the popping action attracts curious wipers to a slender plastic-bodied fly suspended from the cork.

Another effective technique is to cast with a tandem-jig setup. Tie a ¼-ounce jig in a loop about 2 feet up the line; tie another ¼-ounce jig to the end of the line. When a hybrid grabs one jig, others often give chase in a competitive frenzy. When they see the other jig, they grab it. Use monofilament of at least 12-pound test; otherwise, if you hook two fish, they could pull against each other and snap the line. The tandem-jig technique is not recommended for large hybrids.

With any of these techniques, cast into the swift water, then retrieve fast enough to keep the lure running a few inches below the surface. If this retrieve doesn't work, slow down and let the lure sink deeper.

Wipers are also stocked in Ross Barnett Reservoir. These fish migrate upstream in spring, about the same time wipers are moving into the tailrace. The most productive area of the upper river is from Ratliffs Ferry to the low-head dam. Wipers tend to school immediately below the dam, but you'll also find them below sharp bends in the river, usually around logs or brush.

To locate the fish, cast a Rat-L-Trap or other vibrating plug using a medium-power spinning or baitcasting outfit with 8- to 10-pound mono. Once you find the fish, switch to a lighter outfit with 4- to 8-pound mono and cast with ⅛- to ¼-ounce jigs with soft plastic or bucktail dressings.

Wipers school by size, so if you're catching only small fish, you'll probably have to move to find bigger ones.

Fishing is generally best early or late in the day, in cloudy weather, and at normal water stage. When conditions are right, you can catch more than 50 fish in a day.

How to Catch Wipers on Popping Corks

MAKE a long cast to reach wipers in midriver. Using the weighted cork, you can cast up to 150 feet.

RETRIEVE by snapping your rod, reeling down quickly to take up the slack, then snapping again.

SNAP your rod hard enough to throw water, and reel fast enough to keep the fly near the surface.

Pearl River:
Crappies

A newcomer to the Pearl River might get confused when asking about crappie fishing. When the locals say the white perch are biting, they really mean white crappies. If they say just "crappies," they could mean spawning male white crappies, which are darker than the females, or black crappies.

But once you get the terminology straight, you can enjoy some topflight crappie fishing on the Pearl, and on a lot of other southern rivers. Crappies in the Pearl average about a pound, and 2-pounders are not uncommon. White crappies are much more plentiful than blacks.

As in most waters, crappies bite best in spring, when they congregate for spawning. Starting in late February, crappies swim into sloughs off the main channel. They move farther back in when the water is rising and closer to the main channel when it's falling. They spawn in lily pads in 3 to 5 feet of water, usually in late March.

Not all sloughs along the river draw crappies. The best ones have 6 to 7 feet of water at the mouth, and 10 feet or more in parts of the slough. If the water is only 2 or 3 feet deep at the mouth, crappies will probably not spawn in the slough.

Around spawning time, a long cane pole or extension pole with 8- to 14-pound mono is needed for dabbling small jigs or minnows into openings in the pads. If you try to cast into the pockets, you'll snag the pads constantly. Many anglers use a small cork to suspend the jig or minnow off the bottom, experimenting with depth settings until they find the fish.

To cover more water, scull or use an electric trolling motor to move your boat slowly, always into the wind for better boat control. As you move along, try a pocket in the weeds or brush for a few seconds, then lift the bait or lure straight up and drop it into another. Keep moving and varying your depth until you find a concentration of fish. Then anchor or tie off to a tree so you can work the area thoroughly.

In mid-April, the crappies begin moving out of the sloughs and are difficult to locate. Some think they move into the reservoir; others believe they stay in the river, but may be scattered or suspended where anglers are unlikely to catch them. In any case, you're not likely to catch many big crappies in the river during the summer. But you can catch smaller ones in deep outside bends.

Crappie fishing in the upper river is best from the upper end of the reservoir to the low-head dam. Another good location is the Ross Barnett tailrace. From January into May, you'll find crappies in eddies adjacent to the main channel.

How to Catch Crappies Around Spawning Time

LOOK for crappies in deep lily pad sloughs. The pads offer excellent overhead cover for both the adults and newly hatched fry. Normally, you'll find the fish in 3 to 5 feet of water.

LOWER your jig into pockets between the pads. Fish one pocket for a few seconds, then move to another. For best action, attach your jig with a loop knot so it hangs horizontally and swings freely.

LURES AND RIGS for crappies include: (1) bobber rig with a size 6 hook and a small minnow hooked lightly through the back, (2) Slater's Jig, and (3) Whatta Jig.

UNSNAG your jig from a tough lily pad stem by reeling your rod tip down to it, then pushing downward with the rod to dislodge the hook.

Pearl River:
Catfish

When Pearl River anglers talk about "tabby cats," they're not discussing their favorite pets. Tabby cats are actually flathead catfish, the largest of the Pearl's three catfish species.

Channel and blue catfish in the Pearl run 2 to 3 pounds; flatheads, 8 to 10. Channels predominate in the upper reaches; blues in the tailrace. Flatheads are comparatively scarce. The tailrace produces the biggest cats, including blues up to 67 pounds and flatheads up to 75.

Fishing in the upper river differs considerably from that in the tailrace. You'll need different tackle, different rigs and even different baits.

UPPER RIVER. When the Pearl begins rising slowly following a spring rain, blues and channels in the upper river start to bite. Fishing is tough if the water gets too muddy, but slightly murky water is good. The action slows when the water begins falling. Few flatheads are caught in spring.

Channels and blues hang around the mouths of cuts or on sandy points in the main channel, usually at depths of 3 to 12 feet. Anchor or tie up to a snag upstream from your spot, and use a medium-heavy spinning or baitcasting outfit with 17-pound mono and a slip-sinker rig (opposite page). Bait up with nightcrawlers, catalpa worms or fresh chicken livers. Cast downstream, prop up your rod and wait for a bite. If nothing happens in a few minutes, try another spot.

Catfishing in the upper river is slow in summer, but you can catch some fish by working the edges of bars on inside bends. Use a slip-sinker rig baited with worms or whole crayfish. To avoid the summertime heat, some anglers fish at night. The action is slower then, but the fish run bigger.

Fall is the time for flatheads in the upper river. You'll find them in deep holes along outside bends and steep banks, especially if the holes have plenty of woody cover. Flatheads are nocturnal, so night fishing is best.

For flatheads in the upper river, most anglers prefer a stiff baitcasting rod with 20-pound mono. Use the same rig as for channels and blues, but substi-

How to Cast-Net for Shad

ATTACH the line to your left wrist. Grasp the lead line and center ring with your right hand; the lead line again with your left.

THROW the net with a sweeping sidearm motion. If thrown properly, the net should open into a full circle. Let the net sink, but pull the line to close the net before it reaches bottom; otherwise, it may snag. Pull in the net, and dump the baitfish into a pail (inset).

tute a bigger hook, up to 8/0. Bait up with a 4- to 6-inch sunfish hooked through the back.

Fishing for channels and blues in the upper river also picks up in fall. They'll be on the same sandy points as in summer.

TAILRACE. You can catch cats in the Ross Barnett tailrace year around, but fishing really heats up in March, with blues providing most of the early-season action. Flatheads start biting later, usually in late May. Surprisingly, the tailrace produces few channel cats. Fishing in the tailrace is best when the water is stable or falling slowly.

Most blues are caught within 300 yards of the dam. They take refuge from the current in the eddies created by boulders and chunks of concrete. To reach these midriver lies, you'll need an outfit that will cast up to 100 yards. Most tailrace anglers use 12- to 15-foot surf rods with big spinning reels loaded with line to the rim of the spool. The boulders and concrete chunks make for lots of snags, so it pays to spool up with 20- to 30-pound mono.

A double-dropper rig (below) allows you to fish with two baits at the same time. If snags are a big problem, use a float to keep your bait just off the bottom. For blues, shad strips are a good choice in April and May, live crayfish in June, catalpa worms and sunfish heads in July and August, and big grasshoppers in September. For flatheads, try a live sunfish or shad hooked under the dorsal fin. As in the upper river, flatheads bite best at night.

FLATHEADS can be landed by grabbing the lower jaw and pressing down on the tongue area to partially immobilize the fish. A novice should not attempt to land flatheads this way without a leather glove.

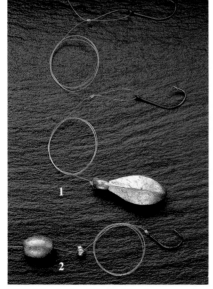

RIGS include: (1) double-dropper rig, tied as shown with 3/0 hooks and 4-ounce sinker; (2) slip-sinker rig, with size 2 hook and 1-ounce sinker.

CATFISH BAITS include: (1) shad strip; (2) grasshopper hooked through abdomen and out behind head; (3) nightcrawler; (4) catalpa worm hooked through head and out middle; (5) chicken liver; (6) sunfish; (7) crayfish hooked just ahead of tail, through body and out below head.

Northern Smallmouth Streams

One of the best-kept secrets in the northern states and southern Canada is the prime stream fishing for smallmouth bass

The northcountry is laced by thousands of small to medium-sized smallmouth bass streams that offer anglers an exceptional fishing opportunity. Within easy reach of millions of anglers, these streams receive surprisingly light fishing pressure.

As in most other parts of the country, fishermen in the North are lake-oriented. Because there are so many lakes, and access to them is easy, anglers tend to bypass the streams.

Most northern smallmouth streams have water that is relatively clear and unpolluted, and a fish population that also includes walleyes and northern pike. The majority flow through forested country, so they are immune to most of the problems afflicting streams in agricultural or urban areas. Because the wooded shorelines keep streambank erosion to a minimum, the bottom has plenty of clean sand and gravel for spawning and food production.

The main problem in fishing these streams is access. Most lack well-developed launching sites, so you may have to slide a small boat or canoe in at a road crossing. And once you're on the stream, you'll have to contend with shallow sandbars and riffles.

Another problem is learning which streams have the best fishing potential. Often, these streams are fished only by local anglers who don't divulge much information. But the state or provincial natural-resources agency may have some good recommendations based on current survey information. They may even direct you to the portion of the stream with the highest fish counts.

St. Louis River, Minnesota

Case Study:
St. Louis River, Minnesota

The St. Louis River is a picturesque, mid-sized smallmouth stream in northeastern Minnesota. It originates in Seven Beaver Lake, then flows on for 190 miles to the western tip of Lake Superior, near Duluth, Minnesota.

Used heavily for logging in the 1800s, the St. Louis was an important route for early traders and explorers because it connected the Great Lakes with the Mississippi River. After a trip up the East Savanna River, a tributary of the St. Louis, travelers portaged 7 miles to the headwaters of the Savanna River, which took them into the Mississippi.

Along its course, the St. Louis undergoes dramatic changes. The upper river flows through wild country, with few farms or other developments. Black bears, moose and even timber wolves frequent the area. The upper 40 miles of the river averages only 60 feet in width; the gradient is high and there are many shallow class 1 and 2 rapids that are impass-

able with a fishing boat. Then, the river flattens into a very slow, meandering stretch extending downstream another 85 miles to Floodwood.

While there is some good fishing in these upper reaches, fishing is best in the 33-mile reach from Floodwood downstream to Cloquet. This zone has several class 1 and 2 rapids, but there are long fishable reaches in between with slow to moderate current and no dams. Despite the easy navigability and good fishing for bass, walleyes and channel catfish, you'll find few anglers.

Below Cloquet, the gradient becomes much steeper. Five dams create a series of small lakes along the river's course. From Cloquet to the Thomson Dam, there is one class 3 and many class 2 rapids, which are impassable in a normal fishing boat. Then, in a mile-long stretch below the Thomson Dam, the river plunges violently through a rocky gorge, dropping more than 200 feet. This is class 6 water. Besides being unnavigable, these lower reaches have little access, so fishing is minimal.

Below the Fond du Lac Dam, the river's character again changes dramatically. Instead of being confined to a definite channel, it winds through an

St. Louis River Habitat

DEEP POOLS are prime catfish haunts, but also hold some walleyes, northern pike and smallmouth bass.

ROCK OUTCROPS along shore attract walleyes and smallmouths if there is deep water nearby.

LILY PAD BAYS are ideal for northern pike, but they also draw good-sized smallmouth bass.

RAPIDS with deep-water pockets

ROCKY POINTS adjacent to deep

estuary that in some places is 1½ miles wide. The main fishing attraction is a seasonal walleye run from Lake Superior. Fishing is best from the time the season opens around May 1 through mid-July. The estuary also produces big northern pike, crappies, bluegills, channel catfish, smallmouth bass and an occasional muskie. In spring and fall, anglers pick up a few trout and salmon.

Most fishing on the upper and middle reaches of the St. Louis is done from 12- to 14-foot semi-V aluminum boats or jon boats with 5- to 15-hp, short-shaft outboards. However, many anglers prefer canoes and some even use float tubes.

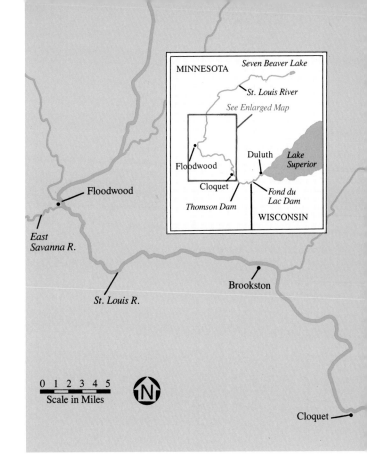

St. Louis River Physical Data (at Brookston)

Average width	200 ft
Average depth	3.5 ft
Gradient	moderate
Clarity	3 to 4 ft
Color	coffee stained
Discharge (cubic feet per second)	1,850
Winter low temperature	32° F
Summer high temperature	82° F

EDDIES that form below point-bars make good resting spots for walleyes and smallmouths.

WEED EDGES along the main channel may hold smallmouths and walleyes, but the fish are scattered.

LOGJAMS provide good smallmouth cover and, on occasion, produce big northern pike.

ROCK PILES in midstream, either exposed or submerged, yield walleyes and smallmouth bass.

LARGE BOULDERS with a deep eddy below them often produce one or two big smallmouths.

CHUTES, where water funnels rapidly through a constriction, make good feeding spots for smallmouth bass.

St. Louis River:
Smallmouth Bass

When you walk along the rocky banks of the St. Louis, you'll see crayfish scurrying everywhere. With this much good bass food, it's not surprising that smallmouths are plentiful.

Besides the abundance of natural food, the river also has plenty of natural smallmouth cover in the form of big boulders, rock outcrops along shore, logjams and weedbeds. There's also man-made cover such as bridge pilings and rock piles that were used to tie off rafts of timber during the logging days.

In most years, snowmelt and cool weather keep the river too high and cold for good smallmouth fishing until early June. When the river drops to normal stage, water clarity improves and the fish concentrate in predictable locations. As a rule, fishing is best from late July through October, assuming the water is at low or normal stage. Time of day is not important, but sunny days are usually best.

Most St. Louis River smallmouths run from 1 to 2 pounds, but when conditions are right, it's possible to catch fish over 4. They're found in many different kinds of spots, but all have one thing in common:

an eddy with faster current nearby. Seldom will you find them where the water is uniformly slack.

To fish smallmouths effectively in the St. Louis, you must be able to recognize the types of spots that hold fish and learn the techniques for fishing each of them.

Local experts use the "hit-and-run" approach to smallmouth fishing. As they run the river, they stop to make a few casts at each likely spot they encounter. Often they carry several rods rigged with different lures to avoid having to rerig for different presentations. Smallmouths are usually aggressive biters; it doesn't pay to spend a lot of time in one spot trying to entice them.

Live bait is seldom necessary to catch smallmouths on the St. Louis. The trend is toward catch-and-release, and fish caught on live bait may be hooked too deeply to survive.

When fishing is tough, however, you may do best by fishing with leeches, crawlers or crayfish, either on a jig or split-shot rig.

A good tackle selection includes a medium-power, 5½- to 6-foot baitcasting outfit with 8-pound mono for crankbait fishing; and a medium-light, 7- to 8-foot spinning outfit with 4- to 6-pound mono for jig and spinner fishing. For live-bait fishing, carry a similar spinning outfit rigged with a split-shot and size 4 or 6 hook.

Smallmouth-Fishing Tips

UNSNAG baits and lures more easily by using an extra-long rod. With a longer rod, you can reach out much farther, giving you a better angle of pull to free your hook from the rocks where smallmouths are often found.

CATCH crayfish using a small-mesh dip net (shown) or a minnow seine. Where crayfish are plentiful, simply scrape the net over the bottom. Otherwise, turn over rocks in a riffle and hold a seine just downstream.

HOOK a small crayfish, 1½ to 3 inches long, in the back using a size 4 hook. Push the hook in one side of the shell and out the other. If you hook the crayfish in the tail, you'll miss more fish.

LURES AND RIGS include: (1) Ugly Bug and leech, (2) Super Vibrax, (3) dropper rig with Phelps Floater and crawler, (4) Shad Rap, (5) Fat Rap.

FAN-CAST a rocky point using a spinner. Retrieve slowly enough so the lure can sink into the crevices between the rocks.

ANCHOR below a rock pile; work both sides and the downstream eddy using a jig-and-leech combo. If snags are a problem, add a slip-bobber.

TOSS a spinner past a boulder, then retrieve it through the downstream eddy. After covering the eddy, try a cast upstream of the boulder.

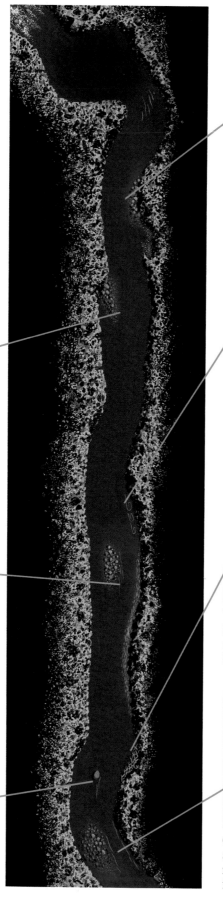

WORK a medium-running crankbait over a rock outcrop. Cast to shore; reel rapidly so the lure bumps the rocks, giving it an erratic action.

POSITION your boat downstream of a point-bar; cast into the eddy using a floater baited with a crawler or leech on a split-shot dropper rig.

WORK a logjam with a spinner by keeping your rod tip high and reeling fast enough to keep the lure from sinking and snagging the logs.

CAST a shallow-running crankbait across a chute. Angle casts upstream; reel immediately to reach bottom before the lure washes downstream.

St. Louis River:
Northern Pike

When the walleyes or smallmouths suddenly stop biting, it could mean that a big northern pike just cruised into your spot. That's your cue to grab a pike rod and start casting.

Northern pike are found throughout the river, except in the headwaters area. They're most numerous in the middle reaches. They prefer slow-moving water, so you'll find them in deep pools, around logjams, and in large eddies. The best pike spots have submerged weeds, such as river pondweed, a type of narrowleaf cabbage.

Few St. Louis River anglers actually fish for northerns, but they catch a good number while fishing for other species. The pike run 4 to 5 pounds, but the river has produced brutes weighing more than 20. Good-sized pike can be found in the middle reaches and in the estuary.

Northerns bite most anytime, from late spring through late fall, as long as the river is not too high. The action is fastest in midday, when fishing for walleyes and catfish is slow.

If you're going to fish specifically for northerns, use a medium-heavy spinning or baitcasting outfit with 10- to 12-pound mono. The most consistent producer is a large bucktail spinner, but pike will also hit spoons, jigs, crankbaits or practically any flashy lure.

LURES for northern pike include: (1) Mepps Giant Killer, (2) Daredevle, (3) ¼-ounce twister-tail jig, and (4) Shad Rap. Always attach your lure to a wire leader, either braided or solid.

How to Bobber-Fish the Rapids

ANCHOR well upstream of the rapids, then let out enough rope to put your boat within easy casting distance. Try to find a section of rapids with fishable water on either side of the boat.

CAST a bobber rig baited with a nightcrawler or leech to the side of the boat, then let the rig drift through the rapids. If the hook snags up too often and pulls the bobber under, set the bobber to fish shallower.

110

St. Louis River:
Walleyes

If you think walleyes are sluggish fighters, you haven't tangled with one in the St. Louis River. The fish have adapted to life in fairly swift current, and they have considerably more power and stamina than a typical lake walleye.

St. Louis River walleyes aren't particularly big, but they're plentiful. On a good day, you might catch two dozen averaging 1½ pounds. There is a chance for a big walleye, however; each year, the river produces a few in the 8- to 11-pound range.

Walleyes bite best from mid-July until late August, but you can catch them into November. Normally, the water is too high for good fishing early in the season, but spring fishing can be good when the water is low. High water slows fishing later in the season, too. The fish bite best early and late in the day, but they often hit all day long when skies are overcast.

There are some walleyes along the entire river, but excepting the spring run in the estuary, fishing is best in the middle reaches. Walleyes use much the same habitat as smallmouths, and you'll often catch one while fishing for the other. Although walleyes spend more time in slow current, they move into fast water to feed, sometimes into rapids only a foot or two deep.

Catching walleyes in the rapids can be difficult, because practically anything you cast will snag almost instantly. But St. Louis River experts have come up with a solution: bobber fishing (photos below).

The hit-and-run approach used for smallmouths (p.108) also accounts for a lot of walleyes. For rapid-fire casting, most anglers use crankbaits, floating minnow plugs, and spinners tipped with a nightcrawler. Sometimes, however, you must take a more deliberate approach. When walleyes are in 4- to 10-foot pools, for instance, they probably aren't feeding, but you may be able to catch a few by slowly retrieving a nightcrawler harness across the bottom.

Use the same rods, reels and line for walleyes as you would for smallmouths. To minimize snagging, many veteran anglers prefer the long spinning rods shown on p.107.

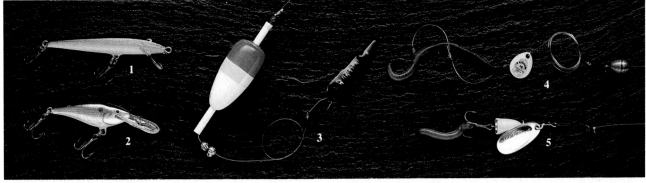

LURES AND RIGS include: (1) Original Floating Rapala, (2) Shad Rap, (3) slip-bobber rig with size 6 hook and a leech, (4) Northland Crawler Harness with a ¼-ounce egg sinker, (5) Super Vibrax tipped with a nightcrawler.

KEEP your rod tip high so your line doesn't drag in the water. If it forms a belly, you'll have trouble hooking the fish. When the bobber goes down, wait a second or two, make sure the line is tight, then set the hook.

TRY different drifts until you cover the entire section of the rapids. From the same boat position, you can easily cover a swath 25 feet from either side of the boat, for a total coverage of 50 feet or more.

111

St. Louis River:
Catfish

When the sun goes down, St. Louis River channel cats go on the prowl. You may be able to catch some in midday, but fishing really picks up at sunset. Normally, the cats bite well until about an hour after dark, then the action tapers off. But at times, they bite all night long.

Channel cats in the St. Louis run good-sized; 3- to 5-pounders are common, and it's possible to catch fish up to 15. The river has no other catfish species.

Catfish inhabit the middle and lower reaches of the St. Louis, including the estuary, but are not found in the extreme upper portion. To find the fish, look for holes at least 10 feet deep, especially if there is a riffle just upstream. Cats rest in the holes in midday, then move shallower to feed in the evening. Another good spot is deep water near a midstream rock pile. You'll also catch cats in rapids and swift runs.

If the river is not too high in spring, you can catch cats as soon as the water warms to the mid-50s, which is usually in mid-June. Fishing slows during spawning time, normally in late June, but picks up again in early July. They continue

RIGS AND BAITS include: (1) slip-sinker setup with size 4 hook, barrel swivel, and ½-ounce egg sinker. Hook (2) live or crushed minnows through the lips, (3) scaled cutbait through the skin. Gob on (4) 2 or 3 crawlers, hook (5) chicken livers through the thickest edge, and mold (6) softened Ivory soap around the hook.

How to Fish a Hole

ANCHOR your boat crosswise to the current at the upper end of a hole. By anchoring this way, it's easier for two anglers to fish the hole at once.

LOB-CAST your bait downstream. Try the deepest part of the hole in midday; fish the edges at night as cats move shallower to feed.

PROP UP your rod, take up slack, and watch the tip closely. When you detect a bite, open the bail, wait a few seconds, then set the hook.

to bite through the summer, and you can catch some fish until the water temperature drops below 50° F in late fall. Cats seem to bite best when the river is rising or falling slowly, but the action slows down during a fast rise.

Cats in the St. Louis will bite on just about any kind of bait. When fishing rapids and runs, it's not unusual to catch them on fast-moving lures, such as crankbaits. They'll bite on a wide variety of stinkbaits, and even on a softened ball of Ivory soap molded around the hook. But natural bait, including minnows, nightcrawlers and chicken liver, is most reliable.

Four- to five-inch minnows can be fished alive, but they'll often catch more cats if you crush them to expose the entrails. Larger baitfish should be filleted, scaled and cut into 1½-inch squares about ¼ inch thick. Fresh chicken liver works well, although it may work better if you let it ripen in the sun for a few days. Natural bait is usually fished on a slip-sinker rig.

There's nothing complicated about fishing for cats. You can catch them from an anchored boat or from shore. Using a medium-power spinning outfit with 8-pound mono, toss out the bait, prop up your rod, and wait. Usually, the wait is not too long.

Canadian Trophy Pike Rivers

*These remote Canadian rivers offer pike fishing
equal to any on the continent*

Every fan of TV fishing shows has watched anglers winching monster pike from remote Canadian waters. The slashing strike and powerful run of a big northern, along with the wilderness setting, stir the blood of all freshwater fishermen.

Most of these giant pike come from lakes; rivers have received much less attention, but in some regions offer even greater trophy pike potential.

Nobody knows how many trophy pike rivers wind through the Canadian wilderness. Even the provincial conservation officials aren't sure — surveying all these rivers would take more time and money than their budgets allow.

Suffice it to say that the pike-fishing potential in these rivers is unlimited. The problem, of course, is

getting there. Most of the rivers flow through nearly uninhabited, roadless areas where the only access is by floatplane. Only a few of these rivers have full-service resorts that cater to fishermen.

As a rule, the harder it is to reach the river, the better fishing will be. While all of these waters can produce pike from 20 to 30 pounds, very few can continue to yield fish of this size in the face of heavy fishing pressure. Pike in remote waters are easy to catch because they seldom see a lure. They grow slowly because of the limited food supply and short growing season; a 20-pounder might be 20 years old. All of this means that a good population of big pike can be fished down quickly.

The most common way of fishing these remote rivers is to operate from a camp that provides basic

needs, such as boats, motors, gasoline, food and lodging. Generally, you'll find better fishing as you get farther from the base camp, so some camps set up outposts 10 to 20 miles away. This way,

Pym Island Camp, Attawapiskat River

anglers have access to water that gets less fishing pressure. They can stock up with food and gas at the main camp, fish their way to the outpost where they spend the night, then continue on the next day without returning to base.

Some pike rivers can be fished by floating with a canoe or rubber raft. Canoe route publications, available from some Canadian natural-resources agencies, provide good information on launching sites, camping areas and take-out spots. They also point out dangerous rapids and show portage routes around them. Some also contain information on physical features, such as depth and current speed, that can be valuable to anglers. If no put-in and take-out sites exist, the only option is to fly in all necessary equipment and set up camp.

Besides trophy pike, many of these rivers offer outstanding walleye fishing, in terms of both numbers and size. Other species sometimes found include whitefish, lake sturgeon, brook trout, and in the Far North, lake trout and grayling.

In any wilderness fishing situation, you should carry survival gear in case of an accident. Should your motor break down, for instance, you'll probably have to spend the night on the river. Take along extra food, matches, warm clothing, a tool kit, a flashlight and insect repellent. In late spring and early summer, when mosquitos and blackflies are worst, carry a mesh headnet, wear light-colored clothing, and set up camp in a well-drained site exposed to the wind.

Case Study:

Attawapiskat River, Ontario

Like most other Canadian trophy pike rivers, the Attawapiskat lies in a remote wilderness area. From its source, Attawapiskat Lake, the river winds 355 miles through the vast Hudson Bay lowlands before emptying into James Bay. The terrain consists mainly of spruce bogs and tamarack swamps. The only settlements along the river are two Indian villages at opposite ends of the river: Lansdowne House on Attawapiskat Lake, and the village of Attawapiskat, just inland from James Bay. Other than a fishing camp at Pym Island, about 100 miles downstream from Lansdowne House, another camp about 120 miles downstream from Pym Island, and a few trappers' cabins, there are no other developments on the river.

The Attawapiskat originates on the bedrock of the Canadian Shield. For the first 60 miles, the river flows over granite bedrock. For the next 90 miles, as the river drops off the shield onto the Hudson Bay lowlands, it flows over a mixture of bedrock, limestone rubble, sand and gravel. In the lower 205 miles, the riverbed consists of limestone, sand and gravel, with no bedrock. Limestone in the middle and lower reaches increases the calcium carbonate content. So the Attawapiskat, like many other rivers in this region, is more fertile than rivers that flow over the shield for their entire length. This explains the abundance of baitfish and the lush growth of aquatic plants.

The Attawapiskat's water has a light tannic stain, caused by drainage from the surrounding swampland. Despite the stain, the usual clarity is 4 to 5 feet. Heavy rains don't cloud the water much; the swamps act as giant filters, removing most of the silt before it reaches the river.

The river has many rapids, even after it drops off the shield onto the lowlands. Class 2 rapids are found throughout, and at low water, there is one class 3 (near the junction of the Lawashi Channel). The rapids make navigation difficult, so it's advisable to hire a guide or consult with someone who knows the river, at least for your first trip.

Motoring through the rapids

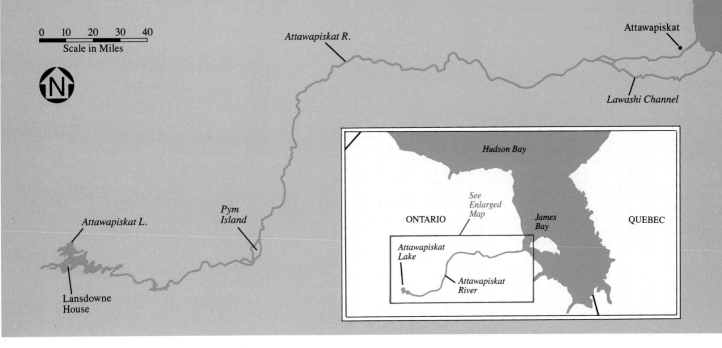

A 14-foot semi-V aluminum boat with a 10-hp outboard is ideal for the Attawapiskat. Some of the rapids require almost the full power of a motor this size to make your way up through them. Don't attempt to run any rapids, however, without scouting them first. Many of the rapids cannot be run with a fishing boat, so you will be confined to fishing stretches between major rapids.

Navigating stretches between rapids can also be difficult. To avoid boulders, you must learn to read the water. In current, you can spot big boulders by looking for boils. But motoring through flat, slow stretches is more difficult because rocks just beneath the surface may not produce a noticeable boil. The best policy is to take it slow and remember the best route for the next time. No matter how careful you are, you're bound to hit some rocks, so you'll need some type of prop guard (photo). It's also a good idea to carry a spare propeller and extra shear pins.

Prop guard

But the quality of the fishing makes up for any problems you may have in navigating the river. The combination of relatively fertile water and light fishing pressure allows the Attawapiskat to produce plenty of big fish. In one recent season, anglers staying at the Pym Island Camp boated 108 northern pike from 17 to 25 pounds, and 88 walleyes from 8 to 14½ pounds. More surprising than the size of the pike is the size of the walleyes. In most rivers this far north, it's unusual to catch a walleye much over 5 pounds.

Legally, you can fish the Attawapiskat year around. But in reality, the season is short. At this latitude, 53° N, the water is too cold for good fishing until late May. After mid-September, the threat of cold, blustery weather keeps most anglers away, although fishing stays good until the river starts to freeze up in early November.

When fishing the Attawapiskat, you'll want to carry a camera. There's a good chance of spotting native wildlife, including moose, woodland caribou, black bear, otter, beaver, marten and bald eagles. To preserve trophy fishing, more and more anglers are photographing and releasing their fish rather than killing them.

Attawapiskat River Physical Data (just above Pym Island)

Average width	880 ft
Average depth	5 ft
Gradient	moderate
Clarity	4 to 5 ft
Color	slight coffee stain
Discharge (cubic feet per second)	11,500
Winter low temperature	32° F
Summer high temperature	75° F

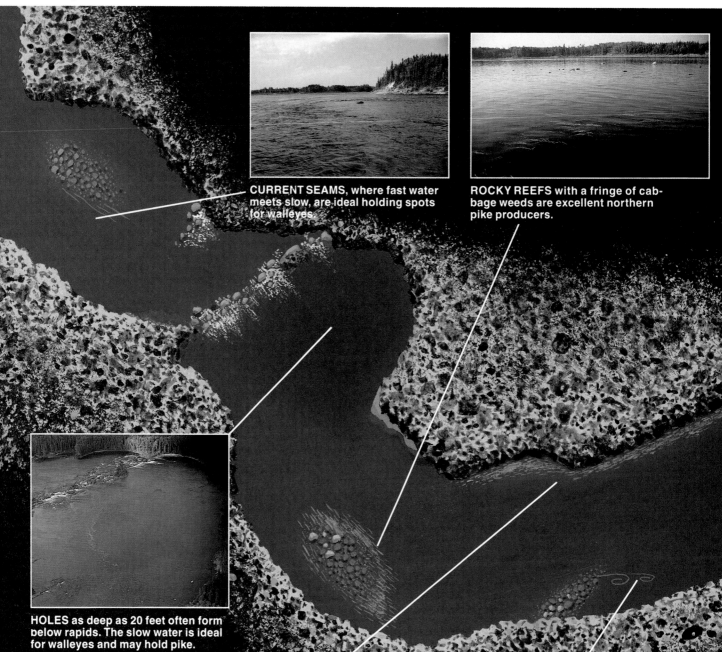

CURRENT SEAMS, where fast water meets slow, are ideal holding spots for walleyes.

ROCKY REEFS with a fringe of cabbage weeds are excellent northern pike producers.

HOLES as deep as 20 feet often form below rapids. The slow water is ideal for walleyes and may hold pike.

WEEDY SHORELINES with cabbage along the drop-off are dependable pike spots in spring. If the drop-off is sharp enough, pike will stay there through summer.

EDDIES below rocky points are excellent spots for northern pike, especially in spring, before cabbage beds have developed.

DOWNSTREAM ENDS of islands with a growth of cabbage are also good spots for pike.

CREEK MOUTHS hold northern pike and walleyes for several weeks after spawning is completed.

DEEP SLOTS with moderate current hold good numbers of walleyes and

CABBAGE BEDS below large boulders are often overlooked, but deep beds

MIDRIVER cabbage beds are the most reliable pike producers in the summer

Attawapiskat River:

Northern Pike

Catching northerns in the Attawapiskat is simple — once you learn where they hang out. They're much less "educated" than pike in heavily fished waters; they'll hit practically any kind of flashy lure you toss at them.

In early spring, pike run up tributary creeks to spawn in flooded shoreline vegetation. They finish spawning in late May, but hang around the lower ends of the creeks or in the creek mouths until mid-June. Then they begin moving away from the creeks, seeking out points next to deep eddies that form along the main shoreline or islands. You'll also find them on sunken islands, especially those with weedbeds remaining from the previous year. The new weed crop has not developed yet.

Once new weeds start to come up, pike move into them. But not just any weeds will do; the fish are very selective. The secret is finding Richardson's pondweed, a type of broadleaf cabbage. There are

Tips for Finding Cabbage Beds

NEW cabbage beds have plants with lush, green weeds and water from 2 to 6 feet deep along the edge.

OLD cabbage beds have plants that are turning brown and dying. They produce only small pike.

SLICK SPOTS on the surface reveal the location of cabbage beds on a breezy day, enabling you to spot the weeds at a distance.

LIGHT RIPPLES in slow-current areas often indicate a cabbage bed just beneath the surface. Sometimes you can see the flowering heads sticking out of the water.

other types of submerged weeds in the river, but they hold only smaller fish.

If you find the right weeds, you'll have no trouble catching pike through the summer. But big pike stay in the weeds only as long as the weeds remain green. If the water is still high when the first beds develop, the weeds may not stay green for more than a few weeks. As the water level drops, weeds that were growing in 5 feet of water are suddenly in only a foot or two. Consequently, they begin to turn brown and die.

Though small pike remain in the dead weeds, big pike move to new weeds that develop in areas that were previously too deep. In fall, usually early September, all the cabbage starts to die off, so pike move deeper or seek cover along the banks.

The downstream end of a weedbed is most likely to hold pike. You'll find fewer fish at the upper ends, and fewer yet along the sides. To better see the weed margins, wear polarized sunglasses.

Another spot likely to hold big pike in summer is the pool below a rapids. The pools draw other fish species, including suckers, burbot, whitefish and perch, all potential pike food. In this situation, the pike may be in deeper water, often 10 feet or more.

Weather and time of day make a big difference in pike-fishing success in the Attawapiskat. As a rule, the pike turn on in cloudy weather, sometimes feeding all day long. They turn off in sunny weather. They bite better in early morning than at midday, and they normally bite again toward evening.

Equipment for trophy pike must be sturdy for casting heavy lures, setting the hook in the fish's bony jaws and horsing them out of the weeds. Choose a 6- to 7-foot heavy-power baitcasting rod with a fast tip, and a matching reel spooled with 30- to 40-pound Dacron line. The reel should have a high gear ratio so you can retrieve fast enough to keep lures from sinking into the weeds. A heavy wire leader is mandatory; a big pike's needle-sharp teeth can shear off heavy mono in an instant.

How to Fish Pike in Cabbage

CURRENT

CAST upstream when fishing in cabbage. The current pushes the stems downstream, so you can cast into slots between the plants without fouling your lure. For best boat control, start at the lower end of the cabbage bed and backtroll slowly upstream alongside the weeds until the entire bed has been covered.

Big bucktail spinners with chartreuse or orange blades are the best all-around pike producers. They work well in spring, when pike are in shallow creeks or on points. They're also effective in summer, when pike are in weedy cover. You can easily keep them riding above the weeds, and if they do foul, a fast sweep of the rod will often clear them. Big spoons and floating minnow plugs also account for lots of trophy pike in shallow cover.

Pike can be moody and stubborn; they'll commonly follow a bucktail or spoon but refuse to strike. When this happens, switch to a minnow plug and twitch it across the surface. The erratic action frequently triggers a strike.

When you're jigging for walleyes below rapids or in deep runs, pike often bite off your lure. If this happens, grab your pike rod and make a few casts with a big crankbait or deep-diving minnow plug. These lures will easily reach depths exceeding 10 feet. And don't be surprised if you hook a trophy walleye while you're at it.

LURES for pike include: (1) Magnum Rapala, (2) Original Floating Rapala, (3) Daredevle, (4) Mepps Giant Killer, (5) M/G tandem spin.

KEEP your rod tip high on the retrieve to prevent the lure from sinking into the cabbage and fouling. Lower the rod when the lure nears the boat.

SWEEP the rod to the side (arrow) at the end of the retrieve. Pike often follow the lure to the boat, and this change of direction sometimes draws a strike.

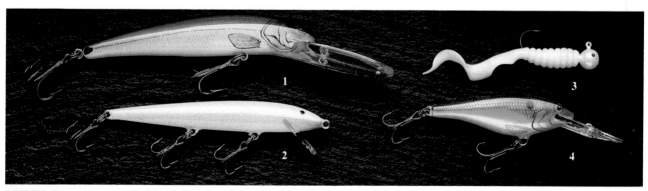

LURES for walleyes include: (1) Bomber Long A, (2) Original Floating Rapala, (3) ¼-ounce Mister Twister Meeny Jig, (4) Shad Rap. When fishing the Attawapiskat, there's always the chance of hooking a big pike, so many anglers use a short wire leader, even when fishing for walleyes.

Attawapiskat River:
Walleyes

It's possible to catch walleyes almost anyplace you drop your line in the Attawapiskat. The fish are in deep, slow-moving stretches, fast rocky runs, and anywhere in between. But most are found in very specific areas.

In late May or early June, the walleyes run up feeder creeks to spawn. They gather below the first barrier, which is usually a rapids or beaver dam. You may have trouble getting your boat upstream that far, but you can often find walleyes in deep pools in the creeks. Some walleyes also spawn below rapids or on gravel bars in the main river.

After spawning, walleyes move into eddies, pools and deep runs in the main river. They will tolerate a moderate current but avoid swift current. Although the river has water as deep as 20 feet, most walleyes are caught at depths of 5 to 10 feet.

You'll find the biggest concentrations below the rapids, especially if there is a deep pool just downstream. Walleyes remain in these areas through the open-water season.

Regardless of where the walleyes are, they tend to line up along current seams. Below many rapids, for instance, there will be a slack-water zone alongside the fastest water. Often, the water in this zone is actually eddying upstream. With few exceptions, the heaviest concentration of walleyes will be found along the line where fast water meets slow or eddying water.

Most Attawapiskat walleyes are caught by two basic methods: trolling and jigging. Trolling is more

effective for covering long runs; jigging works better in shorter runs, eddies or pools. In spring, you can catch walleyes in and around the creeks by casting floating minnow plugs or medium-running crankbaits.

For trolling, use medium-power baitcasting gear and 8- to 12-pound mono. Troll upstream at moderate speed using minnow plugs or crankbaits that run 5 to 7 feet deep, preferably in orange, chartreuse, or blue and silver. Plugs that run deeper hang up too much. If you do get snagged and break the line, the plug often floats back up so you can retrieve it.

For jigging, use a medium-power spinning rod with a fast tip and a matching reel spooled with 6- to 8-pound mono. Jig vertically while drifting with the current or anchor and cast along current seams using ¼- to ⅜-ounce twister-tail jigs in white or chartreuse.

Jigging has one major advantage over trolling: you can work a spot much more thoroughly and often entice half-interested walleyes to strike. Trolling will take the active fish, but the others will ignore a fast-moving plug.

When jigging, it's usually best to anchor upstream of the area you want to fish, especially when the bottom is rocky. This way, you can angle your casts downstream and retrieve upstream so the current helps your jig ride over the rocks. If you get snagged, you can let your line belly downstream; then a swift sweep of the rod creates a downstream tug on the jig that usually pulls it free.

Walleyes seem to have a feeding schedule opposite that of northern pike. They bite best in sunny weather, and midday fishing is usually better than morning or evening. You'll catch the most walleyes in late May and early June; the biggest ones in late August and early September.

How to Jig-Fish Below the Rapids

FIND a deep slot by motoring across the river below the rapids while watching your depth finder.

ANCHOR along a current seam so you can fish the zone between the fast and slow water.

CAST downstream and work the jig back in small hops. If you snag up, release some line, then tug sharply.

Western Corridor Rivers

Corridor rivers serve as a highway for anadromous fish and provide good fishing for resident species

An anadromous fish spends most of its life at sea. Then, as it begins to feel the spawning urge, unknown clues help it find its way into the same river where it hatched years earlier. In some western streams, the fish must struggle through wild rapids, leap waterfalls, and bypass dozens of tributary streams that could lead it off course. Finally, it turns into the right tributary, then wriggles on its

belly through inch-deep water to reach the same spawning riffle where its life began. In some cases, the journey may span 1,000 miles.

Impossible as this sounds, millions of anadromous fish, including steelhead, chinook salmon and white sturgeon, once performed this feat each year in the West's "corridor" rivers. The term *corridor* means that the river serves as a passageway for migratory fish on their way to spawn in the upper reaches or in a smaller tributary.

Most corridor rivers are too warm to support trout year around, except in the upper reaches. But they have warmwater fish populations that often include smallmouth bass, walleyes, crappies and catfish.

While resident fish species are thriving in most corridor rivers, anadromous fish populations now face an enormous problem. As the West's population grows, so does the need for electricity, and the tremendous power-producing capacity of these major rivers has not been ignored. Hydroelectric dams have transformed many rivers into a series of lakes, blocking the runs of anadromous fish. And despite the considerable damage already inflicted, many more dams are being planned.

Some steps have been taken to help the fish reach the spawning areas, but these efforts have not been entirely successful. Fish ladders allow migratory fish through the dams, but they won't allow passage of fish the size of sturgeon.

Biologists discovered that staggering numbers of anadromous fish were being killed in the tailwaters of the dams as they tried to pass upstream. Tiny air bubbles driven into the water as it cascades over a dam cause nitrogen supersaturation. The bubbles wind up in the bloodstream of fish, in effect, giving them the bends.

To eliminate the supersaturation problem, many of the dams were modified by adding concrete slabs to smooth the flow and reduce the amount of turbulence.

Even if the fish get through all the dams and spawn successfully, the young would probably not make it back to sea on their own. Up to 15 percent of the fish were being killed at each dam as they passed through the turbines.

The downstream migration is aided in several ways: the young fish are captured and transported to the sea on barges or trucks, flushed over the dams by the release of a large volume of water, or diverted through a bypass system that keeps them out of the turbines. These creative measures have stabilized anadromous fish runs in many rivers, and some runs have even showed a dramatic improvement. But others have continued to dwindle, often for reasons biologists do not fully understand.

One possible explanation for declining runs is loss of genetic purity. To compensate for deteriorating runs, there has been widespread stocking of steelhead and salmon. Often, brood fish from one stream were used to supply young for a different stream. Then, those fish bred with the natural fish, producing offspring not as well suited to the stream.

The rehabilitation of the West's corridor rivers has been one of the largest fisheries restoration projects ever attempted. While there are some signs of success, a great deal more work is needed.

Snake River, Idaho and Oregon

Hells Canyon

Case Study:

Snake River, Idaho, Oregon & Washington

The Snake starts as a mere trickle from a canyon wall in the high wilderness country north of the Teton Range. It rapidly gains strength, merging with more than 40 other rivers before it finally joins the Columbia at Pasco, Washington, 1,000 miles from where it began.

Along the way, a series of 17 hydroelectric dams impede the river's flow. The major free-flowing portion of the river, the Hells Canyon area, offers the best fishing. From the Hells Canyon Dam, the prime fishing zone extends 108 miles downstream to Lewiston, Idaho.

Hells Canyon got its name from early explorers. As they stood at the lip of the mile-deep canyon, one reportedly gazed at the raging river below and remarked, "What a hellhole!" The name stuck.

The deepest gorge in North America, Hells Canyon averages 5,500 feet in depth from the rim to the water's surface. Confined between these steep canyon walls, the river rushes powerfully along a course interrupted by dozens of awe-inspiring rapids.

Upper Hells Canyon, from the dam down about 16 miles, has the most challenging water. There are several class 4 rapids, and at high water, one class 5 — a roaring torrent called Granite Creek Rapids. The water flattens out somewhat in the lower part of the canyon, although there are still plenty of class 2 and a few class 3 rapids. As you approach Lewiston, the water is flatter yet, with no rapids.

The best and safest way to fish the Upper Hells Canyon area is by high-performance jet boat. Snake River guides use 25- to 30-footers with twin engines, enabling them to skim over barely submerged boul-

128

ders and power through 8-foot walls of raging white water.

You can also fish from a raft or McKenzie River drift boat, but this method is much more limiting; once you drift past a good spot, the fast current makes it difficult or impossible to get back upstream to fish it again. There is a boat access just below the Hells Canyon Dam; another at Lower Pittsburg Landing, 32 miles below the dam; and another near the mouth of the Grande Ronde, 79 miles below the dam.

Anglers fishing Hells Canyon for the first time are advised to hire a guide, at least for a day or two. Those who want to fish on their own should contact local experts before their trip. Guides, outfitters, Forest Service personnel, lodge owners and other fishermen can give you advice on running the rapids, locating good campsites, and possibly finding good fishing spots.

When fishing Hells Canyon, you'll have to contend with water levels that change throughout the day. Normally, the water is low in the morning because the turbines at the Hells Canyon Dam do not operate at night. But by midmorning, the turbines are running and the river is rising rapidly. The only way to escape the high water and swift current is to motor downstream and get ahead of the rise.

In years past, the Snake River was famed for its outstanding steelhead and chinook salmon runs. The dams, along with excessive commercial fishing by Indians and non-Indians, have nearly decimated the salmon, and the steelhead runs are a fraction of what they once were. But an extensive

Snake River below Hells Canyon

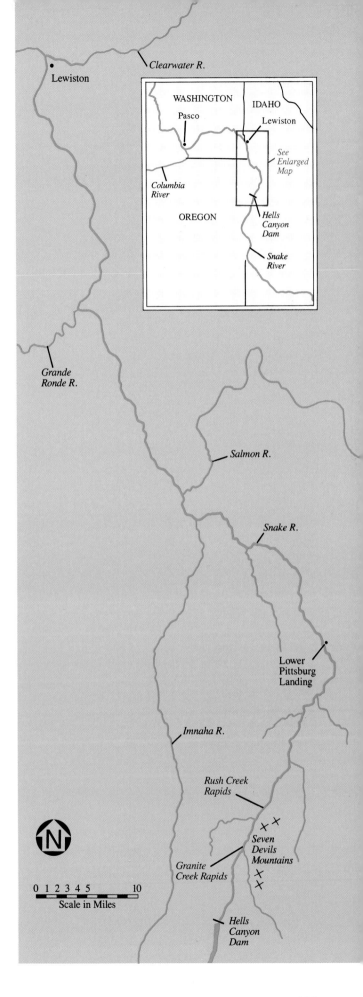

steelhead restoration program has improved those runs considerably, and steelhead fishing can still be good.

Anglers also enjoy good fishing for rainbow trout (actually steelhead that have not migrated to sea). There's a healthy crop of scrappy smallmouth bass, a decent population of channel catfish, and even a few flatheads. For some, the main attraction is the gigantic white sturgeon. Formerly anadromous but now confined between the dams, the sturgeon have adapted well to life in fresh water.

Fishing is only part of Hells Canyon's allure. As you travel through the gorge, you'll see pictographs

Nez Percé pictographs

on the canyon walls, made 6,000 to 8,000 years earlier by the Nez Percé Indians. Although the steep walls often block your view, you'll catch glimpses of the Seven Devils Mountains, especially He Devil, which towers to nearly 9,400 feet. There's also a good chance of spotting mule deer, elk, golden eagles, peregrine falcons, chukar partridge and even Rocky Mountain sheep.

**Snake River Physical Data
(at Lewiston)**

Average width	325 ft
Average depth	18 ft
Gradient	moderate
Clarity	8 ft
Color	greenish tint
Discharge (cubic feet per second)	12,000
Winter low temperature	32° F
Summer high temperature	78° F

Snake River Habitat

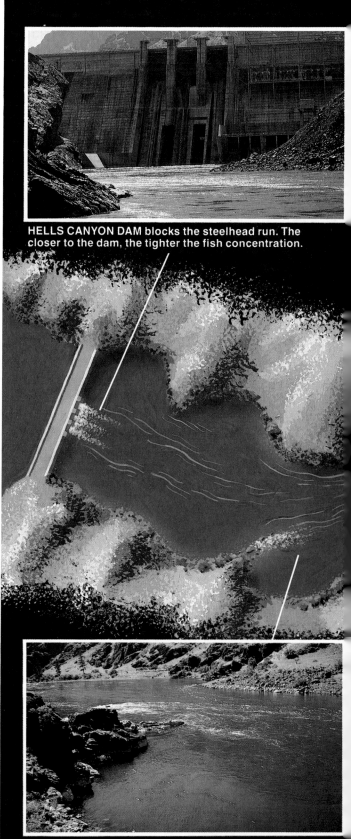

HELLS CANYON DAM blocks the steelhead run. The closer to the dam, the tighter the fish concentration.

DEEP EDDIES below rapids and points are prime locations for smallmouth bass and rainbow trout throughout most of the year.

FAST RIFFLES over gravel bars produce insect larvae and are good summertime feeding areas for rainbows.

TRIBUTARY MOUTHS draw smallmouths in spring. In fall, steelhead move into coldwater plumes below the mouths.

NOTCHES along the canyon walls contain small eddies, which are perfect for rainbows and smallmouths.

SEASONALLY FLOODED BAYS with gravel bottoms make ideal spawning areas for smallmouth bass.

DEEP POOLS below rapids or points hold sturgeon, catfish and, in summer and winter, smallmouth bass.

Snake River:
Steelhead & Rainbow Trout

When you see a sleek, silvery steelhead rocket from the water, making a half-dozen leaps in rapid succession, it's easy to understand why western anglers are so infatuated with this magnificent fish.

Powerful swimmers and world-class leapers, steelhead have been clocked at speeds of 21 mph, the fastest of any fish that swims in fresh water. They easily leap 6-foot waterfalls on their upriver spawning migration.

Some of the West's most famous steelhead rivers, such as the Salmon and Clearwater, empty into the Snake River. During the migration, steelhead must swim up the Columbia and then up the Snake, a distance of 500 miles or more, before entering their home stream.

Although steelhead do not spawn in the Snake itself, they return to the tailrace of the Hells Canyon Dam, where they were stocked. Snake River anglers have a chance to catch these fish, as well as those destined for other steelhead streams.

Stocking has become necessary to build up the steelhead run, but conservation agencies would prefer that steelhead reproduce naturally so their wild nature is preserved. To promote natural reproduction, only stocked fish can be kept; wild ones must be released alive. Stocked steelhead are easy to identify because the adipose fin has been clipped.

Steelhead are stocked as yearlings with the hope that they develop a migratory urge and begin swimming downstream within a few days. The process by which they develop this urge is called *smolting*, and the young fish that migrate are called *smolts*.

But few of the smolts make it back to the sea on their own. The lakelike environments created by the dams present a major obstacle to migration. Because there is very little current to follow, the smolts tend to stray, or even get lost. Even if they make it through one reservoir, they soon encounter another. They retain their migratory urge for about 30 days, but their chances of overcoming all of these obstacles in that amount of time are virtually nil.

Fishways have been installed to allow migrating adults to pass upstream, but for smolts to reach the sea, they must be captured before they pass through the turbines, transported downstream by truck or barge, then released below the Bonneville Dam on the Columbia River. Unfortunately, no more than 40 percent of the smolts are captured. The others become resident rainbows, spending their entire life in the river and never reaching the size or attaining the fighting ability of their sea-going cousins.

The steelhead season on the Snake opens September 1. Migrating fish arrive in early September, but at that time, water in the Snake is normally in the mid-60s. So, many steelhead duck into the Clearwater River, where the water is considerably colder. There they wait for the Snake to cool before resuming their migration. Many also hold in the coldwater plumes from the tributaries. The plumes may extend downstream for several miles below the confluence. By early October, the Snake has cooled into the mid-50s, so many steelhead move out of the Clearwater, and fishing in the Snake starts to pick up. The action peaks from early November through Thanksgiving.

Steelhead caught in the Snake run 5 to 9 pounds. A larger strain of steelhead, fish running 13 to 15 pounds, enters the Clearwater River, and a few of these fish are caught in the Snake below Lewiston.

To locate steelhead, look for areas of moderate current with a bottom of grapefruit- to cantaloupe-sized rocks and water at least 3 feet deep. Usually, the fish lie along a current seam, in the tail of a pool, in troughs on the bottom, or in a "soft spot," a slow area surrounded by fast current.

Once steelhead enter fresh water, they stop feeding, but they occasionally strike lures as an instinctive response or in defense of their territory. Anglers are often frustrated when they see fish tailing all around them but fail to get a single bite. While steelhead fishing can be a challenge, there are many ways to improve your odds and tempt even the most uninterested fish.

One of the deadliest techniques is *backtrolling* (p.134), not to be confused with the same term meaning trolling in reverse. Anglers run a small outboard in forward gear to keep the bow pointed into the current while allowing the boat to slip slowly

LURES AND RIGS for steelhead include: (1) dropper rig, tied with a three-way swivel, a Sammy Special baited with an unpeeled shrimp tail pushed onto one of the two hooks, and a ½-ounce parachute cord sinker on a 6-inch dropper; (2) Wob-Lure; (3) Hot Shot "S.E."; (4) Bomber; (5) Green Butt Skunk; (6) Wooly Bugger.

Prime Locations for Steelhead

TAIL-OUTS of pools (arrow) are classic steelhead locations. The fish rest in the tail-outs after fighting through the rapids.

SOFT SPOTS (arrow) may form above or below points. The current is slower in these areas, so they make good resting spots for steelhead.

CURRENT SEAMS (dotted line) form where a point diverts the flow. Steelhead hold along the margin between the fast and slow water.

How to Backtroll for Steelhead

POSITION your boat at the upper end of a likely run with the bow upstream. While holding the boat's position, let out 60 to 70 feet of line. Mark the line (inset) to show the right amount.

PLACE each rod in a holder, then allow the boat to slip slowly downstream. It's important to let out the same amount of line on each rod so you present a "wall" of lures.

CONTINUE slipping down the run. Some anglers feel that the wall of lures pushes the steelhead down the run, trapping them at the end and forcing them to strike.

Steelhead Fishing Tips

BOONDOGGIN' means casting to the side and upstream of the boat while backtrolling. This technique allows you to cover more water and reach fish that have not been spooked by the boat.

downstream. This technique enables you to hang a lure in the current so it practically brushes the fish's nose, provoking the fish to strike.

Backtrolling gives you excellent boat control. By turning the motor slightly, you can slide sideways in the current without losing ground. Then, by turning the motor back the other way, you can slide back to your original position.

Some refer to the technique as *hotshotting* because the lure most commonly used is a trolling plug called the Hot Shot. It dives rapidly, has an erratic darting action, and comes in the bright colors that steelhead usually prefer.

When fishing is tough, natural bait often works better than lures. One of the most productive live-bait rigs is a floating spinner tipped with a piece of shrimp or a cluster of salmon eggs. This rig is also fished by backtrolling.

An 8½-foot, medium-power baitcasting rod with a soft tip is the best choice for backtrolling. The soft tip allows you to observe the plug's action more easily. Match the rod to a level-wind reel spooled with 10-pound, abrasion-resistant mono. The reel should have a smooth drag.

Other effective methods for steelhead include casting spoons and spinners with light spinning gear, or fly casting with wet and dry steelhead flies.

Steelhead fishing is best when the water is low and the fish are confined to deep pools and runs. Otherwise, they're scattered and difficult to find. Of course, your odds are greatest at the peak of the run. Conservation agencies closely monitor the progress of the run, and the number of fish passing through the Lower Granite Dam is published daily in local newspapers.

SIDE PLANERS allow you to backtroll from shore. Feed 30 feet of line through the planer, secure it to the line, let it plane outward, then walk slowly downstream. You can also use planers to cover more water from a boat.

Weather and time of day are of little importance in steelhead fishing, but the first person of the day to fish a hole or run generally has the best chance.

Although most of the rainbow trout found in the Snake are technically young steelhead, there are major differences in when, where and how you fish the two. You can catch rainbows year around, but the best time is in spring — either in March, before the snowmelt begins, or in late May, when the water starts to clear after the snowmelt. Another good time is September and October, when low flows concentrate the fish and make wading much easier.

Rainbows are found throughout the Hells Canyon area, but the 16-mile stretch from the Hells Canyon Dam downstream to Rush Creek Rapids produces the most fish. These rapids are imposing enough to stop most anglers coming from downstream, so this upper section receives less fishing pressure.

In spring, you'll find rainbows in holes with slow current and water from 3 to 5 feet deep. One of the best locations is a deep eddy alongside a steep cliff or below a rapids. Some remain in the holes through fall, but in hot weather, many move into shallow riffles over gravel bars. They feed in the riffles during the day, then move to deeper runs in the evening. They return to the holes in early October.

Rainbows bite best when skies are overcast and the water is stable or starting to drop. Rising water slows the action considerably.

Most rainbows in the Snake are yearlings that measure 9 to 12 inches. A few hold over to the next year and grow much larger, from 15 to 18 inches and occasionally more than 20. Legally, however, any rainbow over 20 inches is considered a steelhead. If the steelhead season is closed, the fish must be released.

LURES for rainbows include: (1) Wedding Magic spinner baited with a piece of crawler and weighted with a split-shot to run deeper, (2) Shyster, (3) Kastmaster, (4) Elk Hair Caddis, (5) Hare's Ear, (6) Muddler Minnow.

The most popular lure for rainbows is a small, beaded-shaft spinner tipped with a piece of nightcrawler. Squirrel-tail spinners and small spoons also work well. Using a 5½-foot, medium-power spinning rod with 6-pound mono, simply cast into a hole and retrieve slowly. Use the same tackle for fishing the gravel riffles (see below).

Fly-fishing is also effective when rainbows are in the gravel riffles. Dry flies work well early and late in the day, but you'll get bigger trout on nymphs and streamers. Use a 6-weight graphite rod from 8 to 9 feet long with a weight-forward floating line for dry flies; a weight-forward sink-tip for nymphs and streamers.

How to Work a Gravel Riffle for Rainbow Trout

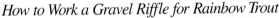

WADE to a position somewhat downstream of the head of the riffle. Using a spinner-worm combo, (1) angle your cast upstream and reel rapidly, gradually slowing your retrieve until the lure is (2) at a right angle to the current. Then, stop reeling and allow the lure to drift to (3) a point somewhat downstream of your position. When the current catches the lure and lifts it to the surface, reel up and make another cast.

Snake River:

Smallmouth Bass

When you mention smallmouth bass, most anglers think of waters in the East. But many western rivers, including the Snake, now have smallmouth populations rivaling those in prime eastern streams.

Although the average smallmouth in the Snake weighs a pound or less, you can catch plenty of fish from 2 to 2½ pounds, especially in spring and fall. The Oregon record smallmouth, 6 pounds, 13 ounces, was caught in Brownlee Reservoir (above Hells Canyon) in 1978.

Like rainbows, smallmouths are found throughout the Hells Canyon area, but the difficult-to-reach upper portion of the canyon offers the best fishing.

Smallmouth fishing in the Snake peaks in April and May, when the fish gather to spawn in slack water above and below points, and in shallow, seasonally flooded bays off the main channel. Some smallmouths run up major tributaries to spawn, and before spawning will concentrate at the mouths.

By June, smallmouths have moved into eddies below rapids and points and into notches along the edge of the main channel. The best eddies have a shallow feeding shelf extending 10 to 25 feet out from shore. Eddies that plunge sharply into deep water seldom produce many smallmouths.

Most fish in the eddies will be found at depths of 3 to 8 feet. They stay in these areas through summer and fall, but when the water warms to the mid-70s, the bigger fish move deeper, often to 15 feet or more. Divers have seen 4- to 5-pound smallmouths in 30 to 40 feet of water in midsummer.

Many of the eddies on the Snake have a fast back-current, sometimes as fast as the main current. There is no advantage for a smallmouth to hold in a back-current this strong, but some part of every eddy is sure to have lighter current. Like a hurricane, an eddy has an "eye," a slacker zone where opposing currents meet, causing the water to rotate. With a little practice, you can quickly spot the eye and locate the smallmouths.

The eddies start to produce bigger smallmouths in mid-September and fishing stays good into mid-

136

INSPECT the entire eddy to find the eye of the eddy (arrow), the area where the current is slowest. Position yourself near the eye, and using a ⅛- to ¼-ounce jig, fan-cast the zone around the eye. Then, move upstream and downstream of the eye until the current becomes too swift, and fan-cast those areas.

October. Then the fish begin moving deeper and become dormant.

Small jigs with marabou or twister-tail dressings will catch smallmouths from spring through fall. Black jigs are proven producers, but green, chartreuse, orange and practically any other color will work. Bounce the jig slowly, or let it rest motionless on the bottom. This no-retrieve method sometimes catches fish when nothing else will.

Smallmouths in the Snake feed heavily on crayfish, so soft-plastic crayfish imitations work well, as do crawfish-pattern crankbaits. Other favorites include vibrating plugs with rattles and split-shot rigs baited with a nightcrawler.

Tackle used for smallmouths is identical to that used for rainbows — a 5½-foot medium-power spinning outfit with 6-pound mono.

Unlike rainbow trout and white sturgeon, smallmouth bass are affected very little by the fluctuating water. Weather and time of day don't seem to matter much in spring or fall, but in summer, fishing is best early or late in the day or when skies are overcast.

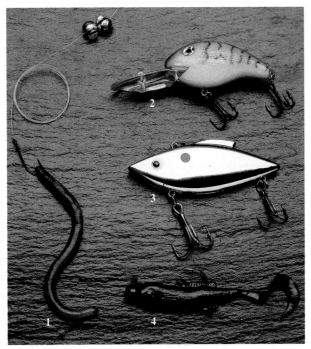

LURES AND RIGS for smallmouths include: (1) split-shot rig with a size 6 hook and a nightcrawler hooked once through the head, (2) Deep Wee R, (3) Rat-L-Trap, (4) Curly Coho Wiggle Tail Jig.

Snake River:

White Sturgeon

Until you see one of these primitive fish, it's hard to imagine how a creature of such massive proportions could exist in a stream not much more than a stone's throw across.

Before the dams on the Snake and Columbia were built, white sturgeon were anadromous, swimming hundreds of miles upriver to spawn, then returning to the sea. An individual female spawns only once every 4 to 11 years, but there were runs of fish each year.

Even though the dams now prevent adults from migrating, the river still holds impressive numbers of resident fish that spend their entire life in fresh water. In some parts of the Snake, sturgeon are successfully reproducing.

White sturgeon grow very slowly. An 8-footer could be 50 years old. Aging studies have revealed that some fish live as long as 82 years. To preserve these relics, only catch-and-release fishing is allowed in Idaho-Oregon waters.

1. RIG a 10- to 12-inch rainbow on a slip-sinker setup tied with a pair of 5/0 barbless non-stainless-steel hooks on an 80-pound mono leader; add a 10-ounce bell sinker above a large barrel swivel. Push a hook through one eye and out the top of the head; the other under the skin ahead of the adipose fin. Slit the belly.

2. DROP the rig into the eye of the eddy, allowing it to reach bottom before motoring into shore. In areas where the river is narrow, you may be able to reach the eye by casting from shore, but it's important to use a sidearm lob-cast so the bait doesn't tear off the hook.

3. MOTOR slowly to shore with the reel in free-spool. Select a landing spot as close as possible to the eye of the eddy, then tie up the boat in such a manner that it can be untied quickly should a sturgeon start a fast run. Lock the reel and place it in a rod holder.

4. PICK UP the rod and watch the tip closely when you think you have a bite. Normally, you'll see the rod tip jerk sharply a few times as the fish is swallowing the bait, then the line will begin to tighten. Lower the rod tip when the fish begins to move off with the bait.

5. SET THE HOOK with a strong upward sweep of the rod. Lock your elbows against your midsection, then use your entire body for leverage; a powerful hook set is necessary because the heavy line and sinker have a great deal of water resistance.

When sturgeon could be kept, their numbers gradually dwindled. Since catch-and-release fishing began in 1970, the sturgeon population has rebounded.

Six- to eight-footers are common in the Snake, and it's not unusual to catch one over 9 feet. Guides report measuring and releasing fish as long as 12 feet. In 1898, a Snake River trotline fisherman hauled in a sturgeon estimated to weigh 1,500 pounds and measure 18 feet.

Landing these huge fish requires heavy saltwater tackle. Experts recommend a powerful 9- to 11-foot rod with a tip light enough to cast live bait without tearing it off the hook. The level-wind reel must have a smooth drag and hold at least 300 yards of 60- to 80-pound mono or braided Dacron line.

Small rainbow trout, 10- to 12-inchers, make ideal sturgeon bait, although most any kind of fresh fish about this size will do. Rig the bait on a double-hook setup (opposite page), then drop it into a deep hole.

A typical sturgeon hole is 30 to 70 feet deep and has a large eddy. These holes usually lie below a rapids, point or sharp bend in the river. Sturgeon are normally found near the eye of the eddy, where the current is slowest.

With a little practice, you can cast your rig into the right spot with your boat on shore, but it's easier to simply drop the rig from the boat, then feed line while taking the boat into shore.

When you hook a good-sized sturgeon, you could easily spend an hour fighting it, and possibly up to four hours. Usually, the fish will stay in the hole where you hooked it, but occasionally one swims through powerful rapids in its attempt to escape. Unless you can untie your boat quickly and follow the fish, its attempt will be successful.

Because a fish this size can easily break 80-pound line, it's important to use hooks that will eventually rust away. A stainless steel hook could remain in the fish's mouth indefinitely and might kill it.

A graph, video or LCR is a valuable tool for locating sturgeon. Not all holes in the river hold sturgeon, but in those that do, the fish are easy to detect because of their size.

After fishing a hole for 15 minutes or so without a bite, reel up and move to another hole. Sturgeon have a ravenous appetite, so they're surprisingly easy to catch. It doesn't pay to wait them out.

Sturgeon will bite all year, but fishing is best in May, when the water recedes following spring runoff. High water makes fishing tough because the current washes the bait out of the right spot. Weather or time of day has little effect on sturgeon fishing.

Tips for Handling Sturgeon

GRASP a sturgeon firmly in the mouth and hold it upside down while removing the hook. In this position, the fish seems to relax rather than to thrash wildly.

MEASURE your sturgeon in the water if you're interested in its weight; it is illegal to remove the fish from the water for any reason. A 6-footer would weigh approximately 85 pounds; a 7-footer, 130 pounds; an 8-footer, 185 pounds; a 9-footer, 250 pounds; a 10-footer, 320 pounds; an 11-footer, 400 pounds; and a 12-footer, 495 pounds.

Great Lakes Tributaries

Recovering fish populations in the Great Lakes mean superb fishing in hundreds of tributary rivers and streams

The rehabilitation of the Great Lakes fisheries is perhaps the greatest rags-to-riches story in angling history. And because many fish from the lakes make annual spawning migrations up tributary rivers and streams, fishing success in these waters has also skyrocketed.

By the early 1960s, the combined effects of excessive commercial fishing, pollution, and invasion of predatory species, such as the sea lamprey, had reduced Great Lakes fish populations to an all-time low. In Lake Erie, for example, the commercial walleye harvest had dropped to about 300,000 pounds per year, compared to almost 6 million pounds annually in the 1950s.

With predator fish in such low numbers, baitfish populations were left unchecked. In Lake Michigan, for instance, alewife populations exploded, causing huge die-offs that left hundreds of tons of the small fish decomposing on beaches. In Lake Superior, the problem was smelt. Although they make good forage, smelt are highly predaceous, feeding on the young of many gamefish species.

Conservationists realized that drastic steps were needed to restore the fisheries. Through a joint effort of state and provincial conservation agencies surrounding the lakes, as well as the federal governments of the United States and Canada, an extensive restoration program was initiated.

Commercial netters were bought out or severely restricted as to where, when and how they could fish. Laws were passed to reduce the amount of municipal waste and industrial pollution entering the lakes, but serious pollution persists. Lampreys were poisoned in spawning streams, but budgets for lamprey control have been reduced, and populations are increasing in some areas.

Innovative salmonid stocking programs have greatly improved the fisheries. Some of the lakes now have trout and salmon fishing rivaling that in the Pacific Northwest. The trout and salmon also control the smelt and alewife populations. Intensive stocking has restored walleye fishing in places such as Saginaw Bay on Lake Huron and Little Bay de Noc on Lake Michigan.

While some problems remain, anglers throughout the United States and Canada are flocking to the Great Lakes and their connecting waters. The salmon and trout fishery gets the most attention, but there's also plenty of interest in walleyes, northern pike, muskies and smallmouth bass.

The rivers and streams flowing into the Great Lakes vary tremendously from region to region, depending upon the terrain. Along the north shore of Lake Superior, for example, are dozens of small, high-gradient streams that draw impressive runs of spawning steelhead in spring, but may go nearly dry in late summer.

Many streams entering southern Lake Michigan are slow and muddy, but they draw spawning salmon in fall and walleyes in spring.

In large, deep rivers, such as those flowing over the Canadian Shield into northern Lake Huron, walleyes swim upriver in fall, stay all winter, and spawn the following spring. So they actually spend more time in the river than in the lake. Some of these rivers also draw northern pike and muskies as well as chinook and coho salmon.

Although Great Lakes tributaries are extremely diverse, they all have one thing in common: big fish. The relatively light fishing pressure and the abundance of forage in the Great Lakes result in some of the largest fish to be found anywhere.

French River, Ontario

Case Study:

French River, Ontario

Named by the Ojibwa Indians for the French explorers and missionaries that traveled its waters in the early 1600s, the French River has played a prominent role in Canadian history.

For more than 200 years, the river was part of the main navigation route between eastern and western Canada. From Montreal, fur traders and other travelers paddled up the Ottawa and Mattawa rivers, across huge Lake Nipissing, then down the French into Georgian Bay of Lake Huron. From there, they could travel west to Lake Superior.

From 1885 to 1910, the river supported one of the biggest logging operations in all of Canada. Often, the river was so clogged with floating logs that boat travel was impossible.

Despite its heavy use, the river today looks much the same as when the early explorers discovered it. In 1989, the French River and surrounding area was designated as an Ontario provincial park, protecting it from future development.

From Lake Nipissing, the French winds its way toward Georgian Bay through a maze of granite-walled channels that expand into mile-wide lakes, then split into narrow passages, or "swifts," barely wide enough for a boat.

Ten miles below Lake Nipissing, the river divides into the Main Channel and the North Channel. Eighteen miles farther downstream, the channels rejoin, then flow 14 miles before joining the Pickerel River, then the Wanapitei. Below Ox Bay, the river splits into three channels, the Eastern Outlet, the Main Outlet, and the Western Channel, all emptying into Georgian Bay.

This simplified description does not convey the true complexity of the French River system. Each channel is connected to bays and backwaters, cross channels connect the main channels, and many of the channels have rapids impassable in ordinary fishing boats. Navigation is also complicated by an abundance of barely submerged boulders.

Although the main channel of the French is only 62 miles long, the total length of all its channels measures several hundred miles.

The Upper French (above the Highway 69 bridge) is much more accessible and heavily fished than the Lower French. Below the bridge is a single boat landing (at Hartley Bay), although there are several lodges accessible by water.

Walleyes are the main attraction in the French, especially in spring and fall, when the river is packed with fish from Georgian Bay. Smallmouth bass and northern pike also have a lot of followers, but the main drawing card for many is the world-class muskie fishing. Other species often caught include crappies, largemouth bass and channel catfish. Occasionally someone lands a huge lake sturgeon. And during the fall spawning run, there's a chance of hooking a chinook, coho or pink salmon.

Because of the lakes along the river's course, you'll need a good-sized boat, preferably a 15- to 17-foot aluminum semi-V. A 35- to 50-hp motor is needed to power through the rapids and maintain steerage. Larger boats may have difficulty maneuvering through the narrow swifts.

French River Physical Data (below Highway 69)

Average width	400 ft
Average depth	30 ft
Gradient	moderate
Clarity	3 to 6 ft
Color	slight coffee stain
Discharge (cubic feet per second)	7,000
Winter low temperature	32° F
Summer high temperature	75° F

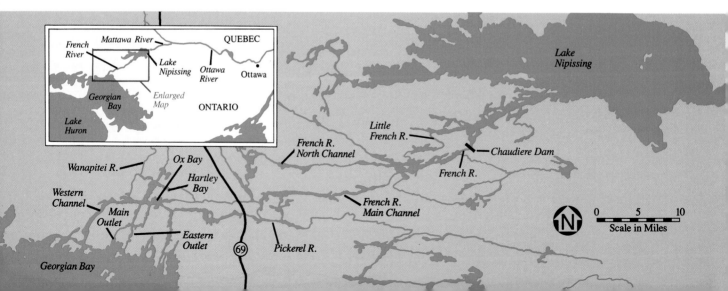

French River Habitat

RAPIDS hold minnows, which draw walleyes and smallmouth bass. They, in turn, attract muskies.

SHALLOW WEEDY BAYS attract large-mouth bass. Crappies often hang along the deep edge of the weeds.

DEEP ROCKY POINTS make good wall-eye spots in summer. Often, the fish are more than 40 feet deep.

NARROWS constrict the flow, causing faster current, which draws walleyes, smallmouth bass and muskies.

WEEDY BREAKLINES hold walleyes in early summer, and they may hold pike, smallmouths and muskies.

WEEDY POINTS with an extended lip are ideal for muskies, pike and, in early summer, walleyes.

POINTS with an extended lip of baseball- to basketball-sized rock are perfect for smallmouth bass.

SWIFTS are narrow passages with strong current. Smallmouths, walleyes and muskies hold just below them.

WEEDY SUNKEN ISLANDS are excellent muskie producers. The best ones top off at 5 to 10 feet.

NIGHT FISHING produces a good share of the big walleyes caught on the French River. Six- to seven-inch

French River:
Walleyes

Statesiders call them walleyes, but to Canadians, they're pickerel. Regardless of how you label them, you'll have trouble finding better fishing on either side of the border.

Some walleyes live in the French year around, but fishing really picks up in mid-September, when walleyes from Georgian Bay start moving upriver. When the run peaks, there will be four bay fish for every resident fish. It's easy to tell the difference: bay fish are dark golden in color; residents, much lighter. The bay fish run 3 to 5 pounds, with a few up to 14. Resident fish are considerably smaller.

The migratory fish are drawn by current, so they congregate below rapids and in narrows, places that

floating minnow plugs in silver or blue are the favorites of local fishermen.

also draw plenty of baitfish. In fall, most of the big walleyes are caught at depths of 15 feet or less, but you'll find smaller ones down to 30 feet.

A plain slip-sinker rig baited with a 2- to 3-inch minnow accounts for most fall walleyes, but a jig-and-minnow also works well. One of the best big-fish methods is trolling the rapids at night with a large floating minnow plug.

Walleyes continue to bite until freeze-up, which is usually in mid-November. They stay around the rapids and narrows through the winter, but treacherous ice makes winter fishing nearly impossible.

The fishing season closes at the end of March, but opens again on the third Saturday in May. For the first week or two of the season, walleyes remain in the rapids where they spawned. But then they begin moving downstream, congregating in narrows with current. Use the same techniques as in fall, working water 10 to 15 feet deep.

After the first week of June, most of the walleyes move to areas with less current. They hold along weedy breaklines and off weedy points, usually at depths of 20 to 25 feet. By mid-June, most anglers

146

How to Troll the Rapids

TROLL a large floating minnow plug below the rapids starting around sunset. Work the eddies along either side of the fast water, then work the current seams between the fast water and the eddies. The plug runs only a few feet beneath the surface, but walleyes spot the silhouette after dark and swim up to strike.

How to Make and Use a Drop-Sinker Rig

TIE on three-way swivel; add dropper with split-shot pinched on and 2-foot, 6-pound leader with size 6 hook. To reduce snags even more, use floating jig head (bottom).

KEEP your line nearly vertical while drifting with the current. Allow the split-shot to touch bottom every few seconds, but don't let the rig drag along the bottom.

LOWER your rod tip when you feel a bite, then set the hook quickly. The line cannot slip through the sinker, so the fish may feel resistance and drop the bait if you wait too long.

switch to nightcrawlers. Normally, fishing stays good into early July.

By mid- to late July, most of the migratory walleyes have moved back to Georgian Bay. Resident walleyes start to go deeper, commonly to 30 or 40 feet, but sometimes to more than 70 feet. You'll find them off steep cliffs and deep rocky points, but reduced walleye numbers and abundant forage make summertime fishing difficult. It stays tough until walleyes from the bay return in the fall.

A 5½- to 6-foot medium-power spinning outfit with 6- to 10-pound mono is adequate for most French River walleye fishing. But snags can be a big problem in the French, especially when fishing around rapids and narrows where current scours the bottom and keeps rocks exposed. In this situation, even 10-pound line won't prevent break-offs, so some anglers use drop-sinker rigs (see above). To keep your hook out of the rocks, you may want to add some type of floater.

The French has fairly clear water, so overcast days with a slight chop usually make for the best walleye fishing. As a rule, the action is fastest early and late in the day.

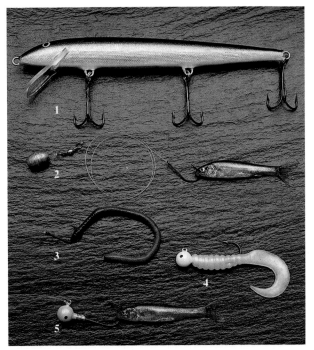

LURES AND RIGS include: (1) Original Floating Rapala, (2) slip-sinker rig with a ¼-ounce egg sinker and a size 4 hook baited with a minnow or (3) nightcrawler, (4) Mister Twister Meeny Jig, (5) jig and minnow.

147

French River:
Muskies

Many muskie-fishing authorities believe that a Georgian Bay tributary will produce the next world-record muskie. And the French is definitely one of the top candidates.

In 1988, a 65-pound muskie was caught in the Moon River, a Georgian Bay tributary about 80 miles south of the French. The French produced a 59-pound, 11-ounce muskie in 1989.

When you're fishing for muskies that commonly top the 30-pound mark, don't expect the action to be fast. Some days you won't get a strike or even a follow, but if you keep working at it, your efforts will pay off.

You can improve your chances by picking your fishing times carefully. The muskie season opens on the third Saturday in June, but the fish feed very little until mid-July. The peak time is mid-September until freeze-up. Some experts believe that muskies bite better around the full moon and dark of the moon than at other times of the month.

Muskies may strike at any time of the day, but evenings are usually better than mornings. Weather is important, too. Cloudy days with a moderate chop make for better fishing than sunny, calm days.

You can find muskies anyplace where weeds border deep water. Milfoil is the most common vegetation in muskie areas, but the type of weed doesn't seem to matter much, as long as there is a drop-off nearby.

Certain spots seem to produce muskies regularly; when one is caught and removed, another moves in. The main ingredient for a choice muskie spot is a large food shelf. Muskies move up on the shelf to feed, then drop into the deep water to rest. The food shelf could be an extended lip off a point or a weedy sunken island.

Muskies behave like northern pike in most ways, but they will tolerate faster water. They often hold in pools below rapids or in narrows with noticeable current. Muskies feed on the walleyes, smallmouth bass, suckers and smaller baitfish that concentrate in these areas.

Another difference between the two species: muskies prefer warmer water than big pike. Small pike stay in the French all year, but the big ones move down to the lower channels of the French or into Georgian Bay, where the water is at least 10 degrees cooler. Muskies migrate much less; most remain in the river permanently.

When a pike spots your lure, it's likely to strike. But a muskie is more inclined to follow, inspecting the lure right up to the boat. When this happens, reel to within a foot of your lure, thrust your rod vertically into the water and sweep it in a figure-eight motion. The rod doesn't bother the fish, which will often come back and strike.

Casting with bucktails and topwater lures is the most productive method when you know there's a fish around the area. But trolling with big plugs accounts for most muskies caught in the French River. It allows you to cover a lot of water and helps you find likely spots that you can later work more thoroughly by casting. Trolling will catch muskies anytime, but it's most effective in summer, when the fish go deeper.

There's always the chance of hooking a 50-pound muskie in the French, so you'd better have sturdy tackle. Most experts prefer a heavy-power 7- to 7½-foot rod with a fast tip and a level-wind reel spooled with 30- to 50-pound Dacron. The long rod improves casting distance and allows you to keep the lure deeper when figure-eighting after a follow. Otherwise, the boat may spook the fish.

As in most other prime muskie-fishing areas, the trend is toward catch-and-release. Should you catch a muskie and wish to release it, bring it to the net as quickly as possible, then try to unhook it in the water using a longnose pliers with a wire cutter. If necessary, cut off the hook points to set the fish free. The hooks can be easily replaced; a trophy muskie cannot.

How to Fish a Bucktail

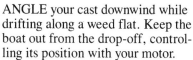

ANGLE your cast downwind while drifting along a weed flat. Keep the boat out from the drop-off, controlling its position with your motor.

KEEP your rod tip high at the start of the cast and reel rapidly to keep the lure from sinking. This way, you can "buzz" it over the weedtops.

LOWER your rod tip and reel more slowly when the bucktail reaches the drop-off. This allows the lure to gradually sink along the weed edge.

LURES for muskies include: (1) Grandma Lure, (2) Jointed Believer, (3) Huskie Devle Jr., (4) Husky Cisco Kid, (5) Buchertail, and (6) Hawg Wobbler. Attach your lure to a solid wire leader with a heavy snap. The snaps and swivels on ordinary braided wire leaders may not be sturdy enough to handle a big muskie.

Muskie-Fishing Tips

CAST a bucktail into the fast water below a waterfall or rapids and retrieve downstream. Work the eddies alongside the fast water as well.

WORK a surface lure over shallow weedbeds, especially in morning or evening. Most other types of lures would foul immediately.

TROLL in the boat's wake using only 40 to 80 feet of line. Muskies don't seem to mind the sound of the motor; in fact, some say it attracts them. Another advantage to trolling with a short line: when a muskie strikes, you can sink the hooks more easily because there is less line stretch.

French River:
Smallmouth Bass

Famed for its outstanding walleye and muskie fishing, the French River is equally good for small-mouth bass. When conditions are right, you can catch 50 bass in a day, with several in the 3- to 5-pound class. In 1988, the river produced a smallmouth weighing 7 pounds, 4 ounces.

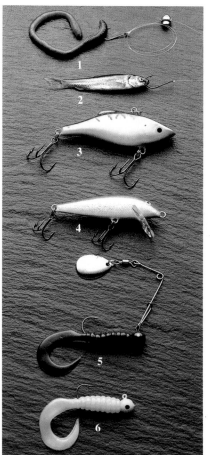

LURES AND RIGS for smallmouths include: (1) split-shot rig baited with a nightcrawler or (2) minnow, (3) Rattl'n Rap, (4) CountDown Rapala, (5) Mister Twister Meeny Spinner-bait, (6) Mister Twister Meeny Jig.

The smallmouth season opens late, the third Saturday in June. This regulation is intended to protect the fish until spawning is completed, which is usually around mid-June. By early July, females have recuperated from spawning and are starting to feed.

You'll find smallmouths throughout the French River system, all the way down into Georgian Bay. They prefer much the same habitat as walleyes, but they're usually a little shallower. Prime locations include eddies below rapids, narrows with current, weedy breaklines and rocky points. You'll find them along the main channels; in bays and backwater lakes off the main channels; and in the "tides" (p. 154), a network of channels, bays and islands around the mouth of the river. The best spots have a bottom of rubble and small boulders.

Most anglers consider August the best smallmouth month. During the day, the fish hold along rocky breaks at depths of 5 to 15 feet. At night, they go shallower, sometimes moving into the weeds to feed.

Smallmouths continue to bite through the fall, but they form tighter schools, which may be difficult to find. Some may be as shallow as 5 feet; others, as deep as 30 feet. If you locate one of these schools, however, you'll have some outstanding fishing.

Live-bait fishing is the traditional method on the French, although artificials are gaining popularity. Most local anglers use a small minnow or a nightcrawler on a plain split-shot rig. Popular lures include small crankbaits, floating minnow plugs, spinnerbaits and twister-tail jigs.

For live-bait fishing or casting small lures, use a light spinning outfit with a 5½- to 6-foot rod and 6-pound mono. For crankbaits and spinnerbaits, a 5½-foot baitcasting outfit with 10-pound mono works better.

Smallmouths bite best when the weather and flow are stable. You can catch them throughout the day, although a slight chop is better than perfectly calm water.

How to Fish a Rapids for Smallmouth

WORK (1) any eddy at the base of the rapids by anchoring and casting. Next, (2) drift along the current seams on either side of the fast current while casting or vertically jigging; (3) fish the back-currents in the same manner. Finally, (4) work any deep hole below the rapids by vertically jigging or slow-trolling live bait.

French River:
Northern Pike

In most waters, pike are homebodies, seldom wandering far from their usual haunts. But such is not the case in the French River. Around ice-out, big pike from Georgian Bay swim up the river to spawn. They stay in the river until early July, when the water gets too warm, then start moving back toward the bay.

You'll find pike from 3 to 6 pounds in the river all year. But most pike fishing takes place in early season, when there's a good chance of catching 15- to 20-pounders. You'll find them in many of the same areas as muskies, usually at depths of 12 feet or less. Lakes off the main channels are more likely to hold pike than are the main channels themselves. Pike seldom hold below rapids or in any area with much current.

By late July, most of the big pike have moved downstream to channels and bays and between islands near the river mouth. In these areas, called the tides (see below) by local anglers, water from Georgian Bay mixes with the river water, keeping it cooler than water in the upper river. Pike stay in the tides through fall.

You can catch big pike using techniques identical to those used for muskies. The same plugs, bucktails and flashy spoons may produce fish, but slightly smaller sizes usually work better. Most pike anglers use medium-heavy spinning or baitcasting gear with 12- to 20-pound mono; others prefer muskie gear. Of course, a wire leader is a must.

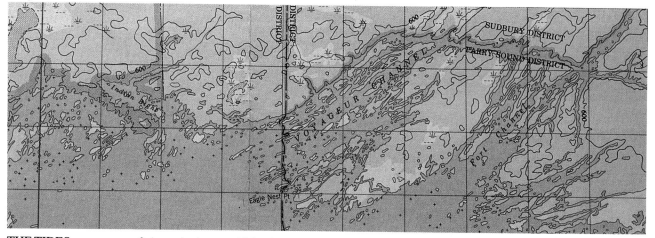

THE TIDES are a maze of channels, bays and islands subject to frequent water-level fluctuations caused by wind-induced currents from the bay. As the water sloshes in and out, it creates an effect similar to an ocean tide.

Other French River Gamefish

LARGEMOUTH BASS live mainly in bays and back-waters. You can catch them by working spinnerbaits over shallow weed flats and along weedy breaklines, or by flippin' plastic worms into the lily pads. The bass run 1½ to 3 pounds, but 5- to 7-pounders have been taken.

BLACK CRAPPIES grow large in the French, with many in the 1- to 2-pound class. You'll find them in the same areas as largemouth bass, but slightly deeper. Most are caught on small twister-tail jigs or a plain minnow fished below a bobber.

Index

A

Agricultural Practices, Effect on Stream Habitat, 28, 39, 103
Alewives, 143
Aluminum Semi-V Boats, 43, 105, 117, 144
American Shad, 67, 68, 83
  See also: Shad
Anadromous Fish, 126, 127, 130, 139
Anchoring, 47-49
  Fishing techniques, 57, 62, 71, 78, 83, 98, 100, 108, 110, 113, 125, 153
  Safety, 33
Army Corps of Engineers, 28, 40, 43, 68
Arrowhead, 70
Artesian Wells, 58
Attawapiskat River (Ontario), 115-125

B

Backtrolling, 48, 122
  As term for slipping, 133, 134
  Photo sequence: How to backtroll for steelhead, 134
Backwaters and Backwater Lakes, 29, 40, 43, 44, 67, 144
  As general habitat, 41, 45, 48, 52, 54, 58-60, 62, 153, 154
  As spawning location; 40, 47, 51, 56, 62
  Fishing techniques, 48, 51, 52, 54, 56, 58, 59, 62
  Formation of, 40, 67
  See also: Rice Fields, Sloughs
Baitfish, 23, 27, 43, 60, 78, 79, 116, 143, 146, 150
  See also specific species of baitfish
Bank Erosion, 28, 29, 86, 103
Bank Fishing, 43, 62, 97, 113
Banks, 27, 41, 84, 85, 100, 122
  See also: Undercut Banks
Barges, 28, 33, 39, 41, 43, 60
Bars, 14, 83, 100, 105, 108, 131
Bass, 86, 104
  Habitat preferences, 10
  Locations in rivers, 69, 89
  See also: Largemouth Bass, Smallmouth Bass, Spotted Bass, Striped Bass, White Bass, Wipers
Bays, 86, 104
Black Crappies, 88
  Current-speed tolerances, 10
  Fishing techniques, 51-53, 84, 98
  Locations in rivers, 84, 98, 155
  Lures, rigs and bait, 99, 155
  Population levels, 84, 98
  Rods, reels and line, 98
  Salt tolerance, 68
  Size in various rivers, 84, 98, 155
  Water-temperature preferences, 19
  See also: Crappies
Blue Catfish,
  Current-speed tolerances, 10
  Daily activities, 79
  Effect of weather on fishing, 79
  Fall locations, 78, 101
  Fishing techniques, 78, 79, 100, 101
  Habitat preferences, 78
  Locations in rivers, 68, 78, 88, 100, 101
  Rigs and bait, 78, 79, 100, 101
  Rods, reels and line, 78, 100, 101
  Salt tolerance, 68
  Size in various rivers, 78, 100
  Spawning activities and locations, 78
  Spring locations, 78, 100, 101
  Summer locations, 78, 100
  Water-temperature preferences, 19
  Winter locations, 78
  See also: Catfish
Blueback Herring, 67, 84
Bluegills, 88, 105
  Current-speed tolerances, 10
  Daily activity, 52, 72
  Effect of weather on fishing, 52, 72
  Fall locations, 52, 72
  Fishing techniques, 51-53, 71-73
  Habitat preferences, 52, 70, 72
  Locations in rivers, 51-53, 70-73

Lures, rigs and bait, 51-53, 71-73
  Population levels, 70
  Rods, reels and line, 52, 72
  Salt tolerance, 68
  Size in various rivers, 51
  Spawning activities and locations, 51, 52, 70, 72
  Summer locations, 72
  Water-temperature preferences, 19
  Winter locations, 52, 72
  See also: Sunfish
Bobber Rigs,
  For crappies, 51, 52, 98, 99, 155
  For northern pike, 58, 59
  For sunfish, 51, 52, 71, 72
  For walleyes, 110, 111
  Photo sequences: How to bobber-fish the rapids, 110-111
  How to fish pockets in the brush, 51
Boils, 14, 117
Boondoggin' for Steelhead, 134
Boulders, 12, 34, 106, 117, 128, 144, 153
  Buoys to mark, 31
  Eddies around, 13, 14, 101, 108
  Effect on current, 11, 14
  Fish location around, 9, 13, 105, 119
  Fishing techniques, 108
Brackish Water, 66, 81
Braided Channels, 24
Branches,
  As cover, 12, 17
  As current break, 17
  Fishing techniques, 62
Breaklines, 145, 146, 153, 155
Bream, 78, 88
  See also: Sunfish
Bridges and Bridge Pilings, 27, 41, 68, 69, 81, 106
  Location of eddies around, 14, 54, 57, 81
Brook Trout, 115
Brush and Brush Piles, 24
  As cover, 26, 51, 62, 72, 91
  As current break, 47
  As spawning habitat, 94
  Fishing techniques, 47, 48, 51, 94, 98
  Photo sequence: How to fish pockets in the brush, 51
Bucktail Spinners, 59, 109, 123. 150, 151
  Photo sequence: How to fish a bucktail, 150
Bulrushes, 70, 72
Buoys, 30, 31
Buzzbaits,
  For largemouth bass, 54, 75-77, 91, 93
  Photo sequence: How to fish a buzzbait, 76

C

Cabbage, 109, 118, 119, 121-123
  Photo sequences: How to fish pike in cabbage, 122-123
  Tips for finding cabbage beds, 121
Canadian Shield, 116, 143
Canadian Trophy Pike Rivers, 114-125
Canals, 69, 70, 75, 83
Cane Beds, 52, 53
Canoes, 30, 34, 35, 88, 103, 105, 115
Carolina-Rigged Soft Plastics, 93, 94
Cast-Netting for Shad, 100
Catalpa Worms, 71, 79, 100, 101
Catch-and-Release Fishing, 107, 117, 139, 141, 150
Catfish, 109, 127
  Current-speed tolerances, 10
  Daily activity, 62, 79, 100, 112
  Effect of weather on fishing, 62, 79
  Fall locations, 62, 78, 100, 101
  Fishing techniques, 62, 78, 79, 100, 101, 113
  Habitat preferences, 62, 63, 78, 112
  Locations in rivers, 40, 41, 44, 45, 62, 63, 69, 78, 89, 100, 101, 104, 112, 131
  Population levels, 62, 67, 86
  Rigs and bait, 62, 63, 78, 79, 100, 101, 113
  Rods, reels and line, 62, 78, 100, 101, 113
  Size in various rivers, 62, 78, 100, 112
  Spawning activities and locations, 41, 62, 78
  Spring locations, 62, 78, 100, 101
  Summer locations, 62, 78, 100
  Water-temperature preferences, 18
  Winter locations, 62, 78
  See also: Blue Catfish, Channel Catfish, Flathead Catfish, White Catfish
Channel Catfish, 78, 104, 130, 144
  Current-speed tolerances, 10, 11
  Daily activities, 62, 112
  Effect of weather on fishing, 62

Fall locations, 62, 101
  Fishing techniques, 62, 100, 101, 113
  Habitat preferences, 62, 63, 112
  Locations in rivers, 62, 63, 68, 88, 100, 101, 105, 112
  Population levels, 62
  Rigs and bait, 62, 63, 100, 101, 113
  Rods, reels and line, 62, 100, 101, 113
  Salt tolerance of, 68
  Size in various rivers, 62, 100, 112
  Spawning activities and locations, 62
  Spring locations, 62, 100
  Summer locations, 62, 100
  Water-temperature preferences, 19
  Winter locations, 62
  See also: Catfish
Channel Markers, 15, 31, 41
Channelization, 28, 29, 39
Channels, 16, 40, 144, 153, 154
Chinook Salmon, 127, 129, 143, 144
Chuggers, 76
Classifications of Rivers and Streams,
  Canadian trophy pike rivers, 114-125
  Great Lakes tributaries, 142-155
  International Scale of River Difficulty, 34, 35
  Midwestern mainstem rivers, 5, 39-63
  Northern smallmouth streams, 102-113
  Southern largemouth rivers, 86-101
  Tidewater rivers, 64-85
  Western corridor rivers, 126-141
Coho Salmon, 143, 144
Cold Fronts, 9, 54, 86
Coldwater Rivers and Streams,
  Fish species in, 18, 19
  See also: Trout Streams
Coldwater Tributaries, 18, 21, 58, 59
Coontail, 54
Cooper River (S. Carolina), 5, 65, 67-85
Corridor Rivers, 5, 126-141
  Defined, 127
Coulee Creeks, 59
Countdown Technique, 52, 83
Cover in Rivers and Streams, 12-17, 41
  Effect on fish populations, 12, 29, 106
  Recognizing good cover, 13
  See also: Overhead Cover
Crankbaits,
  For channel catfish, 113
  For largemouth bass, 54, 55, 75-77, 91, 93
  For northern pike, 109, 123
  For saugers, 49
  For smallmouth bass, 56, 57, 107, 108, 137, 153
  For spotted bass, 94, 95
  For striped bass, 80, 81
  For walleyes, 49, 111, 123, 125
  For white bass, 60
Crappies, 86, 105, 127, 144
  Daily activity, 52
  Effect of weather on fishing, 52
  Fall locations, 52
  Fishing techniques, 51-53, 98
  Habitat preferences, 12, 17, 52
  Locations in rivers, 41, 51-53, 89, 98, 145
  Lures, rigs and bait, 51-53, 99
  Photo sequence: How to catch crappies around spawning time, 98-99
  Rods, reels and line, 52, 98
  Size in various rivers, 51, 98
  Spawning activities and locations, 51-53, 98
  Summer locations, 98
  Winter locations, 52, 98
  See also: Black Crappies, White Crappies
Crayfish, 15, 57, 62, 77, 100, 101, 106, 107, 137
  How to catch, 107
  How to rig, 101, 107
Creeks,
  As general habitat, 58, 85, 121
  As spawning location, 69, 70, 75, 121, 123, 125
Crickets, 71, 72, 84
Culverts, 73
Current, 26
  And formation of undercut banks, 17
  And wing dams, 15, 40
  How cover breaks current, 13, 16, 17, 68, 121
Current Seams, 118, 125, 133, 147, 153
Current Speed, 9-12, 40, 41
  Effect on bottom, 147
  Effect on fish locations, 40, 41, 119
  Effect on water temperature, 19, 20
  Factors that influence, 10, 11, 16, 27, 145
  Tolerances of various fish species, 10
Cut Bait, 62, 79, 113
Cutgrass, 70

Cuts, 40, 88
  As general habitat, 48, 60, 67, 69, 72, 75-77, 84, 85, 89, 91, 94, 95, 100
  Fishing techniques, 75-77, 94, 95, 100
  Photo sequence: How to work the cuts, 75
Cypress Trees, 84, 88, 91

D

Dabbling, 71, 72, 98
Dams, 27, 39-42, 94, 104
  And creation of lakes, 19, 40, 104, 127, 132
  And habitat destruction, 86, 127
  And tidal influence, 66
  Blocking fish migration, 83, 89, 127, 130, 132, 139
  Closing dams, 44
  Eddies around, 16, 41, 60
  Effect on water temperature, 19-21
  Fish locations around, 41, 47-49, 94, 96, 97
  Hydroelectric dams, 67, 127, 128
  Low-head dams, 88, 89, 94, 97, 98
  Navigation dams, 41
  Numbering of, 41
  Safety around, 33
  Surface-draw dams, 20
  See also: Coldwater Draws, Tailraces
Deltas, 15, 42
Dewatering, 28
Ditches in Rice Fields, 67, 69, 70, 75, 76
Docks and Dock Posts,
  And shade, 17, 72
  As cover, 17, 72, 77, 81
  Eddies around, 17
Dredging, 28, 29, 39, 43
Drifting, 49, 60, 62, 72, 79, 125, 147, 150, 153
  Drifting a bobber rig, 110, 111
Drop-Offs,
  Fish locations along, 27, 118, 149
  Fishing techniques, 49
Drop-Sinker Rigs, 101, 108, 133, 147
  Photo sequence: How to make and use a drop-sinker rig, 147

E

Eddies, 9, 12, 33, 141
  As general habitat, 81, 84, 91, 94, 97, 98, 105, 107, 118, 121, 125, 130, 131, 153
  Eye of the eddy, 136, 137, 140
  Fish locations in, 13, 47, 48, 52, 60, 101, 109, 135-137
  Fishing techniques, 49, 101, 108, 125, 137, 140, 147, 151, 153
  Formation of, 13-17, 41, 108, 133
  How to identify, 13, 14
  Photo sequences: How to fish a deep eddy for white sturgeon, 140
    How to work the eye of an eddy for smallmouth, 137
Emergent Vegetation, 41, 70, 72
Erosion, 14, 24, 28, 29, 86, 103
Estuaries, 105, 109, 111, 112
Eye of the Eddy, 136, 137, 140

F

Fall (season), 42
  See also references under individual species
Fallen Trees, 13, 17, 52
Fast Water, 41, 151
  Edges, 52, 125
  Fish behavior in, 11
  Fish location in, 9, 11
  See also: Current, Rapids
Fish Location in Rivers and Streams,
  Effect of changing water level on, 5, 26, 27, 42
  Effect of current on, 11
  Size of fish in relation to cover, 13
  See also references under individual species
Fish Populations,
  Diversity of, 39-41
  Factors that influence levels of, 9, 23, 39
  See also references under individual species
Fishing Pressure, 103, 114, 117, 135, 143, 144
Flathead Catfish, 78, 88, 130
  Current-speed tolerances, 10
  Daily activities, 62, 100
  Effect of weather on fishing, 62
  Fall locations, 62, 100, 101
  Fishing techniques, 62, 100, 101

Habitat preferences, 62, 63
How to land, 101
Locations in rivers, 62, 63, 88, 100, 101
Population levels, 62
Rigs and bait, 62, 63, 100, 101
Rods, reels and line, 62, 100
Salt tolerance, 68
Size in various rivers, 62, 100
Spawning activities and locations, 62
Spring locations, 62, 100, 101
Summer locations, 62, 100
Water-temperature preferences, 19
Winter locations, 62
See also: Catfish
Flats, 150, 155
  As general habitat, 52, 85
  As spawning habitat, 75
Flies, 97, 133-135
  See also: Poppers
Flippin', 51, 54, 155
Float Tubes, 105
Floaters, 108, 133, 147
Floating Spinners, 134
Floats, 51, 52, 72
  See also: Bobbers
Flooded Timber, 41
Floods and Flooding, 28, 39, 86
  Effect on fish location, 26, 58, 131
  Effect on stream course, 24
Flow, 28
  Effect on current speed, 10
  Effect on food supply, 23
Fluorescent Lures, 72, 73
Fly-Rod Poppers, 52
Food Supply, 42
  And fish growth rates, 43
  Effect on fish populations, 9, 106, 143, 147
  Factors that influence, 23, 29, 64, 103
  Fish requirements, 9, 23
  Location, 15, 16, 23, 27, 28, 69, 73, 76, 89, 104, 105, 122, 131, 145
  See also specific types of fish foods
French River (Ontario),143-155
Freshwater Tolerance of Various Saltwater Species, 68

G

Gizzard Shad, 42, 60
Glow-Poppin' for Sunfish, 72, 73
Golden Shiners, 78
Gradient, 10, 11
  And tidal influence, 66
  Effect on gamefish species, 11
  Effect on water temperature, 19
  Of case-study rivers, 43, 67, 88, 105, 116, 130, 144
Grasshoppers, 23, 101
Gravel, 11, 29, 47, 116
  And food supply, 23, 103, 131
  As general habitat, 11, 35
  As spawning habitat, 47, 51, 56, 103, 125, 131
  Fishing techniques, 135
Grayling, 115
Great Lakes, 104, 105, 143, 144
Great Lakes Tributaries, 142-155

H

Herbicides, Effect on Stream Life, 28
Hickory Shad, 83
"Hit-and-Run" Fishing, 107, 111
  Photo sequence: The hit-and-run technique, 108
Holes, 13, 27, 28, 40, 81
  As general habitat, 52, 62, 69, 75, 76, 78, 100, 112, 118, 141
  Fishing techniques, 62, 79, 113, 135, 153
  Formation of, 15, 16, 24, 118
Hotshotting for Steelhead, 134
Hybrids, see: Wipers

I

Ice Fishing, 52, 55, 59, 146
Idaho, 127
  Snake River case study, 128-141
Insects,
  Aquatic, 23
  As fish food, 9, 23, 27, 81
  As predators of fry, 12
  Larvae, 23, 81, 131
  See also specific types of insects

Inside Bends, 100
  Formation of point-bars along, 14
International Scale of River Difficulty, 34-35
Invertebrates, 23, 28, 43
Irrigation, 28
Islands, 24, 153
  Fish location around, 119, 121, 145, 154
  Formation of eddies around, 16

J

Jack Crevalle, 68, 84
Jet Boats, 35
Jig-and-Pig, 54, 55, 57, 76, 77, 91, 94
Jig-Trolling, 48, 49, 85
Jigging Spoons,
  For largemouth bass, 76, 77
  For rainbow trout, 135
  For wipers, 96, 97
Jigs,
  For crappies, 51-53, 84, 98, 99
  For largemouth bass, 54, 76, 77, 91, 93
  For northern pike, 109
  For red drum, 85
  For saugers, 47-49
  For shad, 83
  For smallmouth bass, 56, 57, 107, 108, 137, 152, 153
  For spotted bass, 94
  For spotted seatrout, 85
  For striped bass, 80, 81
  For sunfish, 51-53
  For walleyes, 47-49, 123-125, 146, 147
  For white bass, 60
  For wipers, 96, 97
  Photo sequences: How to jig-fish below the rapids, 125
    How to jig-troll for walleyes and saugers, 48
  Tipping with live bait, 47, 48, 107, 108, 146, 147
  Tipping with pork rind, 54, 55, 57, 76, 77, 91, 93, 94
Jon Boats, 43, 105

K

Kayaks, 35
Kentucky Bass (Spotted Bass), 88, 94

L

Lake Sturgeon, 115, 144
Lake Trout, 115
Largemouth Bass, 88, 144
  Case study of southern largemouth river, 88-101
  Current-speed tolerances, 9-11
  Daily activity, 55, 91
  Effect of weather on fishing, 55, 75, 91
  Fall locations, 54, 55, 76, 91
  Fishing techniques, 54, 55, 75-77, 91-93
  Habitat preferences, 17
  Locations in rivers, 41, 45, 54, 55, 68, 69, 89, 91, 93, 145, 155
  Lures, rigs and bait, 54, 55, 75-77, 91-93, 155
  Population levels, 67
  Rods, reels and line, 55, 75, 91
  Salt tolerance, 68
  Size in various rivers, 55, 75, 91, 155
  Spawning activities and locations, 69, 75, 89, 91
  Spring locations, 54, 75
  Summer locations, 54, 76
  Water-temperature preferences, 19
  Winter locations, 55, 69, 75, 76, 91
Larvae, 23, 81, 131
Lead-Core Line, 49
  Photo sequence: How to lead-line for walleyes and saugers, 49
Leaders, see: Wire Leaders
Leeches,
  As catfish bait, 62
  As crappie bait, 51
  As smallmouth bass bait, 107, 108
  As sunfish bait, 51
  As walleye bait, 110, 111
Levees, 41
Lily Pads,
  As general habitat, 17, 104
  As spawning habitat, 91, 98
  Fishing techniques, 54, 92, 98, 99, 155
  Photo sequences: How to catch crappies around spawning time, 98-99
    How to work a weedless frog, 92

Locks, 40, 41
  Lock-through procedures, 32
Logjams,
  As cover, 105, 106, 108
  Effect on streamcourse, 15, 24
  Fishing techniques, 62, 108
  Formation of, 24
Logs, 24, 26, 27
  As cover, 12, 62, 63
  As navigational hazards, 33

M

Madtoms, 49
Maidencane, 70
Main-Channel Borders, 40, 41, 60
Main Channels, 43, 45, 88, 144
  As general habitat, 40, 41, 44, 47, 48, 52, 60, 62,
    72, 78, 89, 91, 94, 100, 105, 153, 154
  See also: Channels
Mainstem Rivers, 5, 38-63
  Defined, 39
Man-Made Cover, 41
  See also specific types of man-made cover
Markers (Buoys), 31
Marshland, 40
Mayflies, 23
McKenzie River Boats, 35, 129
Menhaden, 78, 79, 81, 85
Midwestern Mainstem Rivers, 39-63
Migration of Fish, 83, 89, 127, 130, 132, 133, 139,
    143, 146, 147
Mile Markers, 31
Milfoil, 149
Minnesota, 39, 103
  St. Louis River case study, 104-113
  State-record black crappie, 51
  State-record channel catfish, 62
  State-record sauger, 47
  Upper Mississippi River case study, 40-63
Minnow Plugs,
  For largemouth bass, 75-77, 91, 93
  For northern pike, 123, 151
  For saugers, 48, 49
  For smallmouth bass, 56, 57, 152, 153
  For striped bass, 80
  For walleyes, 48, 49, 111, 123-125, 146, 147
Minnows, 9, 15, 23, 145
  As catfish bait, 113
  As crappie bait, 51, 52, 98, 99, 155
  As largemouth bass bait, 55
  As northern pike bait, 58, 59
  As smallmouth bass bait, 152, 153
  As walleye bait, 146, 147
  To tip lures, 47, 48, 146, 147
  See also: Baitfish
Mississippi, 86
  Pearl River case study, 88-101
Mississippi River, 28, 31, 39, 104
  Upper Mississippi River case study, 40-63
  Lower Mississippi River, 41
Moon Phase,
  Effect on fishing, 70, 149
  Effect on shad run, 83
  Effect on tides, 64, 65
Muddy Water, 26, 27, 91
  Fishing techniques, 27
  See also: Murky Water, Water Clarity
Mullet, 78, 79, 85
Murky Water, 39, 91, 100
  Effect on feeding patterns, 49
  See also: Muddy Water, Water Clarity
Muskellunge, 105, 143, 144, 152
  Current-speed tolerances, 9, 10
  Daily activity, 149
  Effect of weather on fishing, 149
  Fishing techniques, 150, 151
  Habitat preferences, 149-151
  Locations in rivers, 145, 149-151, 154
  Lures, 150, 151
  Photo sequence: How to fish a bucktail, 150
  Rods, reels and line, 150
  Size in various rivers, 148, 150
  Water-temperature preferences, 19

N

Narrows, 145-147, 150, 153
Navigation in Rivers and Streams, 9, 30-35, 39
Night Fishing, 72, 73, 76, 77, 81, 100, 101, 112, 113,
    146, 147

Nightcrawlers,
  As catfish bait, 62, 100, 101, 113
  As largemouth bass bait, 76
  As rainbow trout bait, 135
  As smallmouth bass bait, 107, 108, 137, 152, 153
  As walleye bait, 49, 110, 111, 147
Northern Pike, 103, 105, 143, 144
  Case study of Canadian trophy pike river, 114-125
  Current-speed tolerances, 9, 10
  Daily activity, 59, 109, 122
  Effect of weather on fishing, 59, 122
  Fall locations, 59, 122, 154
  Fishing techniques, 58, 59, 109, 122, 123, 154
  Growth rates, 114
  Habitat preferences, 17, 109, 121, 122, 154
  Locations in rivers, 41, 45, 58, 59, 104, 105, 109,
    118, 119, 121-123, 145, 154
  Lures, rigs and bait, 58, 59, 109, 123, 154
  Photo sequence: How to fish pike in cabbage, 122
  Population levels, 114
  Rods, reels and line, 59, 109, 122, 154
  Size in various rivers, 58, 109, 114, 154
  Spawning activities and locations, 119, 121, 154
  Spring locations, 58, 118, 119, 121
  Summer locations, 58, 118, 119, 122, 145, 154
  Water-temperature preferences, 18, 19
Northern Smallmouth Streams, 102-113
Notches in Shorelines, 14, 131, 136

O

Ontario, 115, 143
  Attawapiskat River case study, 116-125
  French River case study, 144-155
Oregon, 127
  Snake River case study, 128-141
  State-record smallmouth bass, 136
Outside Bends, 63, 69, 76, 78, 81, 94, 98, 100
  And depth of channel, 11
  And formation of undercut banks, 17
  And location of channel, 10
  And speed of channel, 11
Overhead Cover, 13, 17, 62, 98
Oxbow Lakes and Sloughs, 88
  As habitat, 89
  Formation of, 24, 89

P

Panfish,
  Locations in rivers, 45, 69, 89
  Population levels, 67
  See also individual panfish species
Pearl River (Mississippi), 86, 88-101
Pickerelweed, 70
Piers, 68, 81
  Techniques for fishing, 52, 81
Pike, see: Northern Pike
Pilings, see: Bridge Pilings
Pink Salmon, 144
Pitchin', 55
  Photo sequence: Pitchin' for largemouths, 55
Plankton, 23, 43
Plastic Frogs, see: Weedless Frogs
Plastic Lizards,
  For largemouth bass, 91, 93, 94
Plastic Worms,
  Carolina-rigged, 93, 94
  For largemouth bass, 54, 75-77, 91, 93, 155
  For smallmouth bass, 56, 57
  For spotted bass, 94, 95
  Texas-rigged, 75-77, 93, 94
Plugs,
  For northern pike, 59, 150, 151
  For saugers, 48, 49
  For striped bass, 80, 81
  For walleyes, 48, 49
  For white bass, 60
  See also: Crankbaits, Diving Plugs, Minnow Plugs,
    Propeller Baits, Trolling Plugs, Vibrating Plugs
Point-Bars, 105
  Fishing techniques, 108
  Formation of, 14
Points, 93, 131, 150
  And current, 83, 133, 136, 141
  As habitat, 48, 89, 94, 95, 100, 101, 104, 121,
    145-147, 153
  Eddies created by, 14, 118, 130, 133, 136
  Fishing techniques, 76, 100, 108, 123
Pools, 12
  As general habitat, 48, 94, 104, 108, 122, 125, 131,
    133, 134, 150

As spawning habitat, 125
  Bottom materials, 11
  Fishing techniques, 94, 125
  Formation, 11, 41
  Numbering, 41
  Recognizing, 15
Poppers, 57
  For smallmouth bass, 57
  For sunfish, 52, 72, 73
  Photo sequence: How to fish a wing dam with a
    popper, 57
Popping Corks, 96, 97
  Photo sequence: How to catch wipers on popping
    corks, 97
Pork Rind, see: Jig-and-Pig
Propeller Baits, 151

R

Rafts, 35, 115, 129
Rain, 28, 54, 91
  Effect on fishing, 9, 100
  Effect on rivers and streams, 27, 42, 116
  See also weather references under individual
    species
Rainbow Trout, 130, 133
  As sturgeon bait, 140, 141
  Effect of weather on fishing, 135
  Fishing techniques and lures, 135
  Growth rates, 133
  Habitat preferences, 135
  Locations in rivers, 130, 131, 135, 136
  Photo sequence: How to work a gravel riffle for
    rainbow trout, 135
  Rods, reels and line, 135
  Size in various rivers, 135
Rapids, 24, 104, 110-112, 115-118, 125, 126, 128,
    129, 133, 135, 136, 141, 144, 146, 147, 150, 153
  As habitat, 104, 111, 122, 130, 131, 145
  Difficulty levels of, 34, 35, 104, 116, 128
  Fishing techniques, 110, 111, 113, 123, 125, 146,
    147, 151, 153
  Photo sequences: How to fish a rapids for
    smallmouth, 153
    How to jig-fish below the rapids, 125
    How to troll the rapids, 147
Reading the Water, 9, 11, 13, 33, 117
Red Drum, 68, 84, 85
Red Wigglers, 71, 72
Redbreast Sunfish, 70
  Daily activity, 72
  Effect of weather on fishing, 72
  Fishing techniques, 72, 73
  Habitat preferences, 72, 73
  Locations in rivers, 70, 72, 73
  Population levels, 70
  Rigs and bait, 71-73
  Rods, reels and line, 72
  Salt tolerance, 68
  Water-temperature preferences, 19
  See also: Sunfish
Redear Sunfish,
  Current-speed tolerances, 10
  Daily activity, 72
  Effect of weather on fishing, 72
  Fishing techniques, 71-73
  Habitat preferences, 70, 72, 73
  Locations in rivers, 70-73
  Photo sequence: How to fish shellcrackers at
    spawning time, 71
  Population levels, 67, 70
  Rigs and bait, 71-73
  Rods, reels and line, 72
  Salt tolerance, 68
  Size in various rivers, 70
  Water-temperature preferences, 19
  See also: Sunfish
Redfish (Red Drum), 67, 84
Reels,
  Baitcasting, 55, 57, 59, 62, 75, 78, 81, 91, 94, 97,
    100, 107, 109, 122, 153, 154
  For catfish, 62, 78, 100, 101, 113
  For crappies, 52, 98
  For largemouth bass, 55, 75, 91
  For muskellunge, 150, 154
  For northern pike, 59, 109, 122
  For rainbow trout, 135
  For saugers, 49
  For shad, 83
  For smallmouth bass, 57, 107, 137, 153
  For spotted bass, 94
  For steelhead, 134
  For striped bass, 81

For sturgeon, 141
For sunfish, 52, 72
For walleyes, 49, 111, 125, 147
For white bass, 60
For wipers, 97
Level-wind, 49, 134, 141, 150
Saltwater, 141
Spinning, 49, 52, 57, 60, 62, 72, 78, 83, 100, 101,
107, 109, 113, 125, 134, 135, 137, 147, 153, 154
Surf casting, 97
Reservoirs, 86, 88, 97, 133
Rice Fields,
As general habitat, 67, 69, 72, 75, 76, 78
As spawning habitat, 70, 75
Defined, 67
Fishing techniques, 75, 76, 77
Richardson's Pondweed, 121
Riffles, 103, 107, 112, 127, 135
As feeding areas, 131
Factors that cause, 11
Photo: How to work a gravel riffle for rainbow
trout, 135
Ripples,
As indication of school of shad, 54
As indication of submerged wingdam, 33
As indication of weedbed, 121
Riprap,
And food supply, 81
As habitat, 14, 41, 44, 48, 52
Fishing techniques, 47, 48, 52
River Pondweed, 109
Rock Piles,
And eddies, 15
And food supply, 15
As cover, 41, 81, 106, 112
Fishing techniques, 81, 108
Rocks, 27, 29, 47
And food supply, 23, 81
As habitat, 52, 104-106, 118, 133, 145, 147, 153
Effect on current, 11
Fishing techniques, 52, 53, 59, 108, 125, 147
Rods,
Baitcasting, 55, 57, 59, 62, 75, 78, 81, 91, 94, 97,
100, 107, 109, 122, 125, 134, 153, 154
Cane poles, 52, 53, 72, 98
Extension poles, 52, 53, 71, 72, 98
Flippin', 91
Fly, 57, 134, 135
For catfish, 62, 78, 100, 101, 113
For crappies, 52, 98
For largemouth bass, 55, 75, 91
For muskellunge, 150, 154
For northern pike, 59, 109, 122
For rainbow trout, 135
For saugers, 49
For shad, 83
For smallmouth bass, 57, 107, 137, 153
For spotted bass, 94
For steelhead, 134
For striped bass, 81
For sturgeon, 141
For sunfish, 52, 72
For walleyes, 49, 111, 125, 147
For white bass, 60
For wipers, 97
Saltwater, 141
Spinning, 49, 52, 57, 60, 62, 72, 78, 83, 100, 107,
109, 111, 113, 125, 134, 135, 137, 147, 153, 154
Surf casting, 97, 101
Trolling, 49
Roughfish, 39-41
Rubber Rafts, 35, 115
Runs, 112, 125, 134
Factors that cause, 11
Fishing techniques, 113, 123, 134, 135

S

St. Louis River (Minnesota), 103-113
Salmon, 105, 127, 143
Salt Tolerance of Various Freshwater Species, 68
Salt Water in Coastal Rivers, 66, 68
Sand, 11, 23, 29, 40, 43, 44, 88, 103, 116
Sandbars, 24, 94, 103
Sandy Bottom, 76
As spawning location, 51, 56, 103
Sandy Points, 89, 94, 100, 101
Saugers,
Current-speed tolerances, 10
Daily activity, 49
Effect of weather on fishing, 49
Feeding patterns, 47

Fishing techniques, 47-49
Habitat preferences, 10, 47
Identification, 46
Locations in rivers, 40, 41, 44, 45, 47-49
Lures, rigs and bait, 47-49
Population levels, 47
Rods, reels and line, 49
Size in various rivers, 47
Water-temperature preferences, 19
Schooling,
Of baitfish, 54, 60
Of catfish, 62
Of largemouth bass, 54
Of smallmouth bass, 153
Of white bass, 60
Of wipers, 97
Sculling, 73, 98
Sediment, 16
Effect on current speed, 10, 11
Settling out to create point-bars, 14
Semi-V Aluminum Boats, 43, 105, 117, 144
Shad,
As catfish bait, 62, 79, 101
As forage, 42, 43, 54, 62, 76, 77, 91, 94, 97
Current-speed tolerances, 10
Daily activities, 83
Fishing techniques, 83
Habitat preferences, 83
How to cast-net for shad, 100
Locations in rivers, 83
Lures and rigs, 83
Migrations, 83
Rods, reels and line, 83
Size in various rivers, 83
Water-temperature preferences, 19
See also: American Shad, Gizzard Shad,
Hickory Shad
Shellcrackers, see: Redear Sunfish
Shelves, 81, 94, 136, 150
Shiners, 60, 78
Shrimp, 79, 81, 84, 85, 133, 134
Side Planers, 134
Silt, 11, 23, 24, 27
Slab Spoons, 96, 97
See also: Jigging Spoons
Slack Water, 45, 88, 107, 125
Fish locations in, 9, 11-13, 17, 52, 69, 118, 136
How to identify, 13
Pockets, 9, 12, 14, 15
Vegetation growing in, 17
See also: Backwaters, Sloughs
Sliders, 57
Slip-Bobber Rigs,
For northern pike, 58, 59
For smallmouth bass, 108
For walleyes, 111, 146
Slip-Sinker Rigs,
For catfish, 62, 63, 78, 100, 101, 113
For saugers, 48, 49
For walleyes, 48, 49, 147
For white sturgeon, 140
Slope, see: Gradient
Sloughs, 29, 40, 43, 88, 89
As general habitat, 44, 45, 89, 93, 95
As spawning habitat, 89, 91, 94, 98
Slow Water, see: Slack Water
Small Boats, 43, 88, 103
Smallmouth Bass, 105, 109, 127, 130, 143, 144
As forage for muskies, 150
Case study of northern smallmouth stream, 102-113
Current-speed tolerances, 9-11
Daily activity, 57, 106, 137, 153
Effect of weather on fishing, 57, 106, 137, 153
Fall locations, 57, 136, 137, 153
Fishing techniques, 5, 56, 57, 106-108, 137, 153
Habitat preferences, 12, 56, 107, 136, 153
Locations in rivers and streams, 40, 41, 44, 45, 56,
57, 104, 105, 107, 130, 131, 136, 137, 141, 145,
153
Lures, rigs and bait, 56, 57, 107, 108, 137, 152, 153
Photo sequences: The hit-and-run technique, 108
How to fish a rapids for smallmouth, 153
Population levels, 56, 106, 136, 152
Rods, reels and line, 57, 107, 137, 153
Size in various rivers, 56, 106, 136, 152
Spawning activities and locations, 41, 56, 131,
136, 153
Spring locations, 131
Summer locations, 56, 57, 131, 136, 145, 153
Water-temperature preferences, 19
Winter locations, 131
Smelt, 143
Smolts, 132, 133
Snake River (Idaho, Oregon, Washington), 127-141

Soft-Plastic Lures, see: Plastic Lizards, Plastic
Worms, Weedless Frogs
South Carolina, 5, 65
Cooper River case study, 66-85
State-record blue catfish, 78
Southern Largemouth Rivers, 86-101
Spinner Rigs, 135
Spinnerbaits,
For largemouth bass, 54, 55, 75, 77, 91, 155
For northern pike, 58, 59, 123
For smallmouth bass, 56, 57, 152, 153
For spotted bass, 94, 95
Spinners,
For northern pike, 59, 109, 123, 150, 151
For rainbow trout, 135
For smallmouth bass, 107, 108
For steelhead, 134
For walleye, 111
For white bass, 60
Split-Shot Rigs,
For red drum, 85
For smallmouth bass, 107, 108, 137, 147, 152, 153
For summer flounder, 85
Spoons,
For northern pike, 59, 109, 123, 151, 154
For rainbow trout, 135
For steelhead, 133, 134
Spottail (Red Drum), 84
Spotted Bass, 88
Current-speed tolerances, 10
Fishing techniques, 94, 95
Locations in rivers, 89, 94, 95
Lures and rigs, 94, 95
Rods, reels and line, 94
Size in various rivers, 94
Water-temperature preferences, 19
Spotted Seatrout, 67, 84, 85
Freshwater tolerance, 68
Spotted Sunfish, 84
Spring (season),
Fish locations, 20, 42
See also references under individual species
Spring Holes, 42, 59
Springflow, 18, 19, 27
Springs,
Effect on water temperature, 21, 58, 59
Steelhead,
Current-speed tolerances, 10
Fishing techniques, 133-135
Locations in rivers, 130-134
Lures and rigs, 133, 134
Photo sequence: How to backtroll for steelhead, 134
Population levels, 128-130, 132
Rods, reels and line, 134
Size in various rivers, 133
Stocking Fish, 127, 130, 132, 143
Stratification of Water, 19
Striped Bass, 67, 88
Current-speed tolerances, 10
Daily activity, 81
Fishing techniques, 80, 81
Habitat preferences, 81
Hybridizing with white bass, 88, 97
Locations in rivers, 68, 69, 80, 81
Lures, 80, 81
Population levels, 80, 86
Rods, reels and line, 81
Salt tolerance, 68
Size in various rivers, 80
Water-temperature preferences, 19
Stripers, see: Striped Bass
Stumpknockers (Spotted Sunfish), 84
Stumps, 41, 84, 88, 89, 93
Sturgeon, 115, 144
Location in rivers, 40, 41, 131
See also: White Sturgeon
Submerged Logs and Trees, 26, 41, 51, 63, 72, 88
Submerged Vegetation,
And spawning locations, 51, 121
As general habitat, 41, 45, 52, 109
See also: Weeds
Sucker Minnows, 58, 62, 63, 122, 150
Summer, see references under individual species
Summer Flounder, 67, 84, 85
Freshwater tolerance, 68
Sunfish, 86
As catfish bait, 79, 101
Current-speed tolerances, 11
Daily activity, 72
Effect of weather on fishing, 72
Fishing techniques, 71-73
Habitat preferences, 17, 70, 72
Locations in rivers, 41, 70, 72, 73
Rigs and bait, 71-73

Rods, reels and line, 72
Size in various rivers, 70
Spawning activities and locations, 70-72
Water-temperature preferences, 18
See also: Bluegill, Redbreast Sunfish, Redear
  Sunfish, Spotted Sunfish
Sunken Islands, 121, 150
Surface Baits, 76, 77, 91, 150
Suspended Fish, 72, 98
  Fishing techniques, 52
Swifts, 144, 145

T

Tabby Cats (Flathead Catfish), 88, 100
Tailraces, 88, 132
  As general habitat, 68, 81, 83, 97, 98, 100, 101
  As spawning habitat, 80
  Fishing techniques, 96, 97, 101
Tailspins,
  For spotted bass, 94
  For white bass, 60, 61
Tailwaters, 43, 127
  As general habitat, 45, 47, 52, 86
  As spawning habitat, 60, 86
  Fishing techniques, 47
Texas-Rigged Soft Plastics, 57, 75-77, 93, 94
Three-Way Swivel Rigs, 78, 79
Tides, 64-66, 75, 79, 81, 83, 154
  Effect on fish locations, 64, 69, 72, 75, 85
Tidewater Rivers, 64-85
Tip-Ups, 55, 59
Trees, see: Fallen Trees, Submerged Logs and Trees
Tributaries, 70, 126, 127, 136
  Eddies created by, 15
  Effect on water clarity, 26
  Effect on water temperature, 18, 21
  Fish locations around, 131
  Great Lakes tributaries (case study), 142-155
  Junctions, 15
Trolling,
  Backtrolling, 48
  Jig-trolling, 48, 49, 85
  Locations for, 119, 125
  With lead-core line, 49
  With live bait, 72
  With plugs, 48, 49, 59, 125, 146, 147, 150
Trolling Plugs,
  For northern pike, 150, 151
  For saugers, 48
  For steelhead, 133, 134
  For walleyes, 48
Trotline Fishing, 62
Trout, 105, 115, 127, 143
  Water-temperature preferences, 19
  See also: Rainbow Trout, Steelhead
Trout Streams, 5, 19, 59
Turbid Water, 47
  See also: Muddy Water, Murky Water
Turbines, 127, 129, 133
Turbulence, 33-35, 127
  Effect on water temperature, 19

U

U.S. Army Corps of Engineers, 28, 40, 43, 68
Undercut Banks, 12, 13, 17, 91
Upper Mississippi River (Minnesota,
  Wisconsin), 40-63

V

Vertical Jigging,
  For largemouth bass, 76
  For saugers, 47-49
  For smallmouth bass, 153
  For walleyes, 47, 49
Vibrating Blades,
  For largemouth bass, 54, 76
  For wipers, 96, 97

Vibrating Plugs,
  For largemouth bass, 76, 77
  For saugers, 49
  For smallmouth bass, 137, 152
  For spotted bass, 94
  For walleyes, 49
  For white bass, 60
  For wipers, 96, 97

W

Wading, 135
Walleyes, 103, 104, 109, 115, 127, 143, 144, 152
  As forage for muskies, 150
  Current-speed tolerances, 10, 11
  Daily activity, 49, 111, 125
  Effect of weather on fishing, 49, 111, 125
  Fall locations, 47
  Feeding patterns, 47, 48, 111, 125
  Fishing techniques, 47-49, 110, 111, 125, 146, 147
  Growth rates, 43
  Habitat preferences, 10, 47, 111, 146, 153
  Identification, 46
  Locations in rivers, 40, 41, 44, 45, 47, 104, 105,
    111, 118, 119, 125, 143, 145
  Lures, rigs and bait, 47-49, 110, 111, 123-125,
    146, 147
  Photo sequences: How to bobber-fish the rapids,
    110-111
    How to jig-fish below the rapids, 125
    How to troll the rapids, 147
  Population levels, 47, 115, 147
  Rods, reels and line, 49, 111, 125, 147
  Size in various rivers, 47, 111, 115, 117, 146
  Spawning activities and locations, 47, 48, 105, 111,
    119, 125, 143
  Spring locations, 44, 45
  Summer locations, 48, 49, 125, 145
  Water-temperature preferences, 18, 19
  Winter locations, 47
Washington,
  Snake River case study, 128-141
Water Clarity, 9, 26, 27
  Effect on fish activity, 27, 106
  Of case-study rivers, 43, 67, 88, 105, 116, 130, 144
  See also: Muddy Water, Murky Water
Water Fertility, 117
  Effect on food supply, 23, 43
  Factors that influence, 28, 116
Water Temperature, 9, 18-21, 133
  Beaver dams and, 24
  Effect of springs on, 21
  Effect of tributaries on, 17
  Effect on fish species, 18, 19, 106, 112, 113, 136,
    150, 154
  Factors that influence, 17-21, 28
  Of case-study rivers, 43, 67, 88, 105, 116, 130, 144
  Preferences of various fish species, 19
  Seasonal changes, 19, 20
Waterfalls, 126, 132, 151
  Effect on tidal influence, 66
  Fish location around, 16
  Movement of, 24
Waxworms,
  As crappie bait, 51, 52
  As largemouth bass bait, 55
  As sunfish bait, 51, 52
Weedless Frogs,
  For largemouth bass, 91-93
  Photo sequence: How to work a weedless frog, 92
Weeds and Weedbeds, 27, 86, 116
  And current patterns, 16, 121
  As general habitat, 16, 72, 75, 85, 89, 93, 105,
    106, 108, 118, 121-123, 145, 146, 149, 150, 153
  As spawning habitat, 75
  Techniques for fishing, 47, 48, 51, 59, 71-73, 75-77,
    98, 122, 123, 150, 151, 155
  See also specific types of weeds
Western Corridor Rivers, 126-141
White Bass,
  Current-speed tolerances, 10
  Daily activity, 60
  Effect of weather on fishing, 60

Fishing techniques, 60, 61
  Hybridizing with striped bass, 97, 188
  Locations in rivers, 40, 41, 44, 60
  Lures and rigs, 60, 61
  Photo sequence: How to catch surface-feeding
    white bass, 61
  Population levels, 60
  Rods, reels and line, 60
  Sizes in various rivers, 60
  Water-temperature preferences, 19
White Crappies, 10, 19, 88, 98, 99
  See also: Crappies
White Perch, 68, 84
  As local name for white crappies, 88, 98
White Sturgeon, 130
  Current-speed tolerances, 10
  Effect of weather on fishing, 141
  Fishing techniques, 140, 141
  Growth rates, 139
  Locations in rivers, 140, 141
  Photo sequence: How to fish a deep eddy for white
    sturgeon, 140
  Population levels, 139, 141
  Rigs and bait, 140, 141
  Rods, reels and line, 140, 141
  Size in various rivers, 141
  Spawning activities and locations, 127, 139
  Water-temperature preferences, 19
  See also: Sturgeon
Whitefish, 115, 122
Widths of Case-Study Rivers, 43, 67, 88, 105, 116,
  130, 144
Willow Cats, 49
Wind, 75, 86
  Effect on fish behavior, 23
  Effect on water levels, 66, 154
  See also weather information under individual
    species
Wing Dams, 29
  As general habitat, 41, 44, 48, 52
  As navigational hazards, 33
  Defined, 40
  Eddies around, 15
  Fishing techniques, 49, 59
Winter, see references under individual species
Winter Flounder, 84
Wipers, 88
  Current-speed tolerances, 10
  Daily activity, 97
  Effect of weather on fishing, 97
  Fishing techniques, 96, 97
  Habitat preferences, 97
  Locations in rivers, 89, 97
  Lures and rigs, 96, 97
  Rods, reels and line, 97
  Size in various rivers, 97
  Water-temperature preferences, 19
Wire Leaders, 59, 109, 122, 124, 151, 154
Wisconsin, 39
  State-record white bass, 60
  Upper Mississippi River case study, 40-63
Wolf River Rigs, 62, 63
Wooden Pilings, 68, 69
Woody Cover, 72, 75, 77, 94, 95, 100
  See also specific types of woody cover (Brush,
    Docks, etc.)
Worms (Natural), 100
  As sunfish bait, 51, 71
  Catalpa worms, 71, 79, 100, 101
  Red wigglers, 71, 72
  Waxworms, 51, 52, 55
  See also: Nightcrawlers, Plastic Worms